# JOURNEYS

# Practice Book
## Volume 1

### Grade 2

HOUGHTON MIFFLIN HARCOURT
School Publishers

ISBN 10:      0-54-724640-4
ISBN 13:      978-0-54-724640-6

11  0928  17 16 15 14 13 12
4500381598

# Contents

# Short Vowels *a, i*

**Read each word. Draw a line to the picture that it matches.**

**1.** drag

**2.** drip

**3.** fist

**4.** fast

**5.** clip

**6.** clap

# Subjects

- A **sentence** tells a complete thought. It has a naming part and an action part.
- The **subject** is the naming part of a sentence.
- The subject tells who or what does or did something. The subject tells what the sentence is about.

**Children** play spy games.

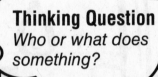

**Thinking Question**
*Who or what does something?*

 **Draw a line under the naming part of the sentence.**

1. Jason sneaks around.

2. Kim looks through windows.

3. My brother writes in a notebook.

4. John reads spy books.

 **Write the naming part from the box to finish each sentence.**

| The cat | Jill |
|---------|------|

5. _____ tells spy stories.

6. _____ purrs on her lap.

# Short Vowels *a, i*

Write labels on the groceries.  Use words from the
Word Bank.

## Word Bank

milk            bran            mints
jam             yams            ham

# Sequence of Events

**Read the selection below.**

It was time to go to school. Jack was on his way to brush his teeth.

Then he saw it. A small green monster was on the bathroom door! Jack said, "Mom! Come here!"

Mom ran into the bathroom. "What is this?"

Dad came. "It looks like a twig that moves. It's an insect called a praying mantis."

"It should not be here," said Mom. She put it on some paper. Then she put it out the back door. Jack saw the bug walk away into the trees. Then Jack went back and brushed his teeth.

**Complete the Flow Chart to show the sequence of events in the story.**

| Event: |
|---|

| Event: |
|---|

| Event: |
|---|

| Event: |
|---|

| Event: |
|---|

Name _____ Date _____

# Short Vowels *a, i*

**Henry and Mudge**
Spelling: Short Vowels *a, i*

Sort the Spelling Words.  Put words with short *a* in one column and words with short *i* in the other column.

| Short *a* | Short *i* |
|-----------|-----------|
| 1. _____ | 7. _____ |
| 2. _____ | 8. _____ |
| 3. _____ | 9. _____ |
| 4. _____ | 10. _____ |
| 5. _____ | 11. _____ |
| 6. _____ | 12. _____ |
|  | 13. _____ |
|  | 14. _____ |

**Basic Words**
1. sad
2. dig
3. jam
4. glad
5. list
6. win
7. flat
8. if
9. fix
10. rip
11. kit
12. mask

**Review Words**
13. as
14. his

Write two more words that have the short *a* and short *i* sounds.  Write the words on the lines.

| Short *a* | Short *i* |
|-----------|-----------|
| 15. _____ | 17. _____ |
| 16. _____ | 18. _____ |

Grade 2, Unit 1: Neighborhood Visit

# Predicates

- A **predicate** is the action part of a sentence.
- A predicate tells what the subject in a sentence does or did.
- The action part of a sentence uses words that show action.

David **hides toys**.

**Thinking Question**
*What does someone or something in the sentence do?*

 **Circle the word or words to finish each sentence.**

1. Sydney _____.

   **looks for clues**        **for clues**

2. Tara _____.

   **house**        **goes into the house**

3. The children _____.

   **act like spies**        **spies**

4. The kids _____.

   **clues**        **follow their clues**

5. Everyone _____.

   **the toys**        **finds the toys**

# Focus Trait: Ideas
# Adding Details

| Without Details | With Details |
|---|---|
| Jackie's dog liked to play. | Jackie's dog liked to chase sticks and play catch. |

**Read each sentence without details added. Then rewrite the sentence, using the details in ( ).**

**1.** The day was rainy. (with a cold wind)

_____

**2.** I took my dog for a walk. (in the park, Duke)

_____

**3.** I got dressed. (in boots, a raincoat, a big hat)

_____

**4.** We walked to a place. (near my school, in the park)

_____

**5.** Duke jumped. (big, into a mud puddle)

_____

Name _____ Date _____

# CVC Words

Finish writing the name of the picture. One syllable is written for you.

1.

pic _____

2.

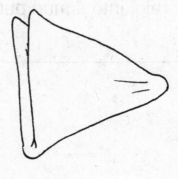

_____ bit

3.

_____ zag

4.

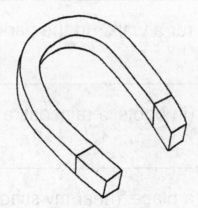

mag _____

5.

ban _____

6.

_____ kin

# Retell Events in Sequence

**Read the selection below.**

Dad stopped the car in the forest. "It's too dark to find our cabin," he told José and Lila.

"Don't worry," said Lila. "We have our flashlights."

José and Lila pointed their flashlights at the trees. All at once, José saw something moving outside the window.

"Dad," said José, "lock the doors! It might be a bear!"

Just then a hand tapped at the car window. Lila and Dad saw a face in the dark.

"I saw your light," the man said. "Are you lost? I can help you find your cabin."

"Good thing we had our flashlights," said José. "They saved us!"

**Answer the questions to retell important events in sequence. Then work with a partner to complete a Flow Chart.**

1. How do José and Lila help Dad find their cabin? Support your answer with details. _____

_____

_____

2. Who does José think is coming up to the car? Why does he think this? Support your answer with details.

_____

_____

Name _____ Date _____

# Short Vowels *a, i*

**Write the Spelling Word that answers each question.**

1. What do you put on bread? _____

2. What do you do with a shovel? _____

3. What do you wear to look like someone else?

_____

4. What do all teams like to do? _____

5. What word tells that something belongs to a boy?

_____

6. What is a tire with no air in it? _____

7. What do you write before you go to the store?

_____

8. What do you do when something is broken? _____

9. What is a word that means *happy*? _____

10. What is a word that means *not happy*? _____

## Spelling Words

**Basic Words**
1. sad
2. dig
3. jam
4. glad
5. list
6. win
7. flat
8. if
9. fix
10. rip
11. kit
12. mask

**Review Words**
13. as
14. his

# What Is a Sentence?

 **Write the subject to finish each sentence.**

1. _____ writes a letter. (Mike, Hold)

2. _____ mails the letter. (Maddie, To)

3. _____ ask for a dog. (Hear, The children)

4. _____ has fun. (Everyone, Throw)

 **Circle the word or words to finish each sentence.**

5. The puppies _____ .

   **ran in circles**          **circles**

6. Henry _____ .

   **dog**                     **found a dog**

7. Mudge _____ .

   **licked Henry**            **Henry**

8. Everyone _____ .

   **patted Mudge**            **patted**

**Lesson 1**
PRACTICE BOOK

# Alphabetical Order

**Put the words in the box in alphabetical order.**

### Word Bank

| collars | straight | floppy | weighed |
|---------|----------|--------|---------|
| big | drooled | dog | curly |
| row | stood | | |

1.
2.
3.
4.
5.
6.
7.
8.
9.
10.

# Proofread for Spelling

Henry and Mudge
Spelling: Short Vowels *a, i*

**Proofread the sign. Cross out the four misspelled words.
Then write the correct spellings on the lines below.**

---

**Welcome to Our Berry Patch!**

We're glid to have you! You can pick your own.
Buy our canning cit, and make your
own jamm. Just ask iff you need help.

---

## Spelling Words

**Basic
Words**

1. sad
2. dig
3. jam
4. glad
5. list
6. win
7. flat
8. if
9. fix
10. rip
11. kit
12. mask

1. _____    3. _____

2. _____    4. _____

**Change the first letter in each word to make a Basic Word.**

5. mix _____

6. sip _____

7. slat _____

8. tin _____

# Contractions

Read each sentence. Write the contraction from the box for each underlined word.

| He's | isn't | It's | can't | I'm | She's |
|------|-------|------|-------|-----|-------|

**1.** <u>He is</u> a big dog.

_____

**2.** <u>I am</u> going to walk him.

_____

**3.** <u>She is</u> going with me.

_____

**4.** That dog <u>is not</u> as big.

_____

**5.** We <u>cannot</u> take too long on the walk.

_____

**6.** <u>It is</u> almost time for dinner!

_____

# Sentence Fluency

---

**Short Sentences**

Pedro collected toys.  Janie collected toys.

**New Sentence with Joined Subjects**

Pedro and Janie collected toys.

---

✐    Read each pair of sentences.  Use *and* to join the two
subjects.  Write the new sentence.

1. Miguel wanted to help kids.

   Anna wanted to help kids.

   _____

2. Mom picked up toys.

   Dad picked up toys.

   _____

3. Tyler wrapped toys.

   Max wrapped toys.

   _____

4. Emma took the toys to the shelter.

   Jack took the toys to the shelter.

   _____

5. The children clapped.

   The parents clapped.

   _____

# Short Vowels *o, u, e*

Word Bank

| tent | skunk | nest | stem |
|------|-------|------|------|
| hump | frog | spot | |

## Write the picture names in the puzzle.

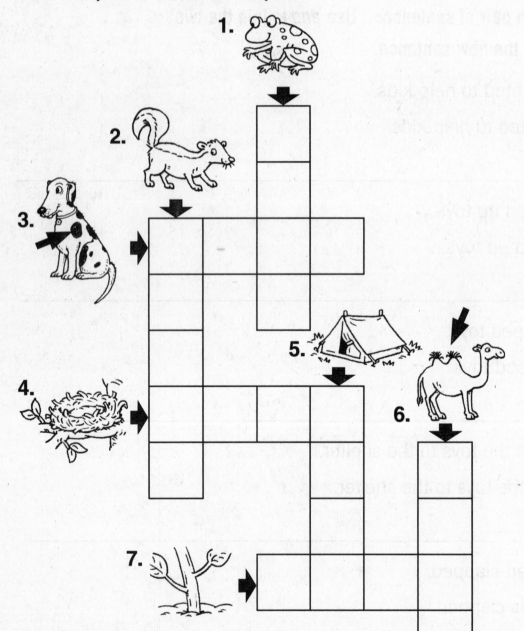

1.
2.
3.
4.
5.
6.
7.

# Is It a Sentence?

- A sentence tells what someone or something does or did.
- A **complete sentence** has a naming part (subject) and an action part (predicate).

Grandma makes a soup.

**Naming part:** Grandma

**Action part:** makes a soup

**Thinking Question**
*What is the naming part and what is the action part?*

 **Underline each complete sentence.**

**1.** Chops peppers.

Harry chops peppers.

**2.** Stirs the soup.

Nan stirs the soup.

**3.** My brother sets the table.

My brother.

 **Circle the part of the sentence that is missing.**

**4.** Grandma and Mama _____.

**naming part**          **action part**

**5.** _____ eat the soup.

**naming part**          **action part**

# Short Vowels *o, u, e*

**Word Bank**

| | | |
|---|---|---|
| stop | bump | left |
| plug | step | up |

## Write the words on the correct signs.

**1.**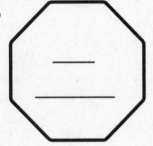

**2.**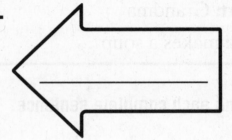

**3.**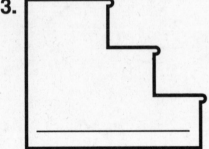

**4.**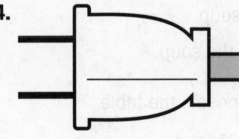

**5.**

**6.**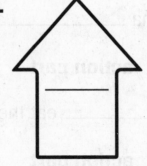

# Compare and Contrast

**Read the selection below.**

My parents are great dancers. They both learned to dance a long time ago.

When my father was young, he went to dance classes in Miami. He was a good dancer, and all the girls wanted to dance with him! He liked to meet new people.

When my mother was young, she would dance in her bedroom. She was very shy.

One day my mother and father went to the same place to dance. He stepped and hopped. She smiled and twirled. They liked dancing together very much.

My parents still dance at our house. They smile and twirl to the beat. When I watch my parents dance, I hope someday to dance as well as they do.

**Think about how the father and mother are different and how they are alike. Then complete the Venn diagram below.**

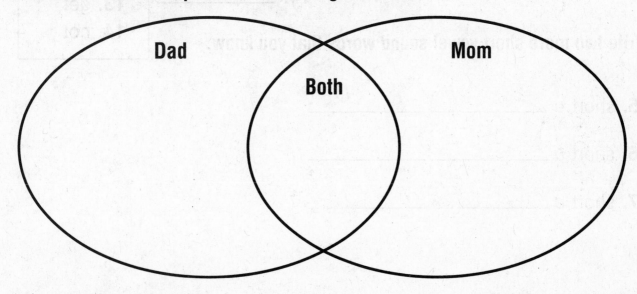

# Short Vowels *o, u, e*

**Short *o***     **Short *u***     **Short *e***

**Sort the Spelling Words by the short vowel sounds *o, u, e*.**

| Short *o* | Short *u* | Short *e* |
|---|---|---|
| 1. _____ | 5. _____ | 9. _____ |
| 2. _____ | 6. _____ | 10. _____ |
| 3. _____ | 7. _____ | 11. _____ |
| 4. _____ | 8. _____ | 12. _____ |
| | | 13. _____ |
| | | 14. _____ |

## Spelling Words

**Basic Words**
1. wet
2. job
3. hug
4. rest
5. spot
6. mud
7. left
8. help
9. plum
10. nut
11. net
12. hot

**Review Words**
13. get
14. not

**Write two more short vowel sound words that you know.**

15. short *o* _____ _____

16. short *u* _____ _____

17. short *e* _____ _____

# Word Order in Sentences

- When a sentence tells something, the naming part comes first.
- The action part of a sentence comes next.

| Incorrect Word Order | Correct Word Order |
|---|---|
| Had a party we. | We had a party. |

**Thinking Question**
*Is the first part of the sentence the naming part?*

 **Draw a line under each sentence that has the correct word order.**

**1.** The family eats snacks.

**2.** Louisa baked a cake.

**3.** Blows out candles Nick.

**4.** The children play games.

**5.** All eat together we.

**6.** Papa opened gifts.

**7.** So much he enjoyed them.

**8.** They ate dessert later.

# Focus Trait: Voice
# Expressing Feelings

| Without Feelings | With Feelings |
|---|---|
| My grandma comes to visit on weekends. | **It's always so much fun when** my grandma comes to visit on weekends. |

**A. Read each sentence. Add words and details to show feelings.**

| Without Feelings | Feelings Added |
|---|---|
| **1.** I <u>liked to</u> help cook dinner. | _____ to help cook dinner. |
| **2.** We <u>talk</u> and work hard. | We _____ and work hard. |

**B. Read each sentence. Then rewrite it to add feelings.**

| Without Feelings | Feelings Added |
|---|---|
| **3.** <u>I live with my family.</u> | |
| **4.** <u>I write stories.</u> | |
| **5.** <u>I had dinner at my friend Adam's house.</u> | |

# Review CVC Words

**Say the picture name. Draw a line between the syllables.**

**1.**

d e n t i s t

**2.**

b o b c a t

**3.**

p e n c i l

**4.**

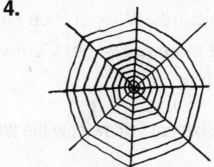

c o b w e b

**5.**

m a s c o t

**6.**

l a p t o p

Name _____ Date _____

Lesson 2
PRACTICE BOOK

My Family
Deepen Comprehension:
Compare and Contrast

# Compare and Contrast

**Read the selection below.**

   Carli and I made books about our lives. I got a green book. I put *I Am Born* on the first two pages. Then I put a birthday on each new page.

   Carli got a purple book. She put her birthdays on the pages, too.

   Next, I added pictures from each birthday. In one picture, my hand is stuck in the cake. Carli put pictures in her book, too. She is playing games and opening presents.

   We showed our books to our families. They told us stories about the pictures. We put their stories in, too.

   I want to add more pages, but Carli wants to keep her book just the way it is.

**Complete the Venn diagram. Show how the two books are the same and different.**

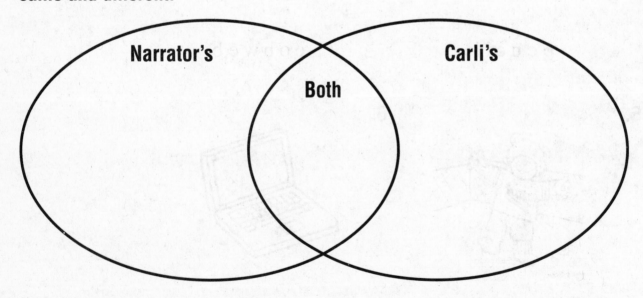

# Short Vowels *o, u, e*

Spelling Words

**Read the first sentence.  Then write the correct Spelling Word to complete the second sentence.**

1. The day was very sunny.  It was _____.

2. The dirt was wet.  We stepped in _____.

3. I often eat a purple fruit.  I eat a _____.

4. My mom wrapped her arms around me.  She gave

   me a _____.

5. I forgot my umbrella.  I got all _____.

**Write the Spelling Word that matches each clue.**

6. A working word that starts with *j* _____

7. You eat this word that rhymes with *shut*. _____

8. This is another word for *stain*. _____

9. It is the opposite of *right*, but is not wrong. _____

10. This sleepy word rhymes with *test*. _____

**Basic
Words**
1. wet
2. job
3. hug
4. rest
5. spot
6. mud
7. left
8. help
9. plum
10. nut
11. net
12. hot
**Review
Words**
13. get
14. not

# Run-On Sentences

✏ Read each sentence. Decide if it is one run-on sentence
or two complete sentences. Circle the correct answer.

1. My cousins played soccer.  Then they went
   swimming.

   **run-on sentence    complete sentences**

2. We play in the backyard we dug holes.

   **run-on sentence    complete sentences**

3. Angel and I like to play together we are best friends.

   **run-on sentence    complete sentences**

4. Uncle Manuel works long hours. He is a doctor.

   **run-on sentence    complete sentences**

✏ Rewrite each run-on sentence into two complete
sentences.

5. My sister learned to dance she took a class.

   _____

6. She practices often every day she goes to the gym.

   _____

7. Sometimes I like to watch her I go with her to class.

   _____

Name _____ Date _____

Lesson 2
PRACTICE BOOK

My Family
Vocabulary Strategies:
Using a Glossary

# Using a Glossary

**Read each glossary entry.  Then use the definitions
to write an example sentence for each word.**

**crown** – a head covering made of gold or jewels

**family** – a group of people who are related

**guitar** – something you play to make music

**house** – a building where people live

**sailor** – a person who works on a ship or boat

**teach** – to show or tell someone how to do something

**1.** sailor

_____

**2.** house

_____

**3.** guitar

_____

**4.** crown

_____

**5.** teach

_____

**6.** family

_____

# Proofread for Spelling

Proofread the journal entry.
Circle the four misspelled words.
Then write the correct spellings
on the lines below.

Today I have a new jub!  I will help Mom wash our
car.  After she washes a dirty sppot, I'm going to wipe
it dry.  Then we're going to have a treat.  Mom made
banana knut bread.  I know I will also get a big hugg.

1. _____     3. _____

2. _____     4. _____

### Spelling Words

**Basic Words**
1. wet
2. job
3. hug
4. rest
5. spot
6. mud
7. left
8. help
9. plum
10. nut
11. net
12. hot

## Use the code to spell the Spelling Words.

| | | | | |
|---|---|---|---|---|
| 1 = a | 2 = b | 3 = c | 4 = d | 5 = e |
| 6 = f | 7 = g | 8 = h | 9 = i | 10 = j |
| 11 = k | 12 = l | 13 = m | 14 = n | 15 = o |
| 16 = p | 17 = q | 18 = r | 19 = s | 20 = t |
| 21 = u | 22 = v | 23 = w | 24 = x | 25 = y | 26 = z |

5. 16, 12 , 21, 13 _____

6. 13, 21, 4 _____

7. 8, 5, 12, 16 _____

8. 12, 5, 6, 20 _____

# Abbreviations

Write the abbreviation on the line for each person's title.

1. We see _____ Garcia when we are sick. (doctor)

2. He plays soccer with _____ Guzman. (mister)

3. We call _____ Vega for a ride home. (missus)

Find the mistakes in titles. Write the new sentence on the line.

4. Dr Perez takes a dance class.

_____

5. Her teacher is mrs Malone.

_____

6. Mr Perez watches the class.

_____

7. mrs. Ramos learns to dance the salsa.

_____

8. mr. Ramos takes the class, too.

_____

# Sentence Fluency

---

**Not Complete Sentences**

Walks me to school.  Uncle Luis.

**Complete Sentences**

My brother walks me to school.

Uncle Luis picks me up.

---

✏️ **Read each word group.  Add a naming part or an action part to each group to make a complete sentence. Use the words in the box.**

---

| | |
|---|---|
| Mom | Aunt Rose |
| brings us gifts | My sister |
| makes me laugh | |

---

1. Uncle Luis _____.

2. _____ helps me do homework.

3. _____ sings to me.

4. Papa _____.

5. _____ cooks me dinner.

# Long Vowels *a, i*

### Word Bank

| time | nice | like |
|------|------|------|
| slice | cake | bake |

**Write the word from the Word Bank that completes the sentence.**

1.

We can

_____.

2.

It takes

_____.

3.

Look at our

_____!

4.

Here is a

_____.

5.

Do you

_____ it?

6.

It is very

_____!

**Lesson 3**
PRACTICE BOOK

**Henry and Mudge
Under the Yellow Moon**
**Grammar:** Statements and
Questions

# Statements

> - A **statement** is a sentence that tells something.
>
> - A statement begins with a **capital letter** and ends with a **period.**
>
> <u>Josh</u> lives in the city.

**Thinking Question**
*Does the sentence tell something, begin with a capital letter, and end with a period?*

 **Write each statement correctly.**

**1.** josh and his family live near the woods

_____

**2.** They have a dog and two goldfish

_____

**3.** josh takes a bus to school

_____

**4.** dad drives to work

_____

**5.** the playground is crowded today

_____

**6.** josh meets many friends

_____

Name _____ Date _____

**Lesson 3**
PRACTICE BOOK

**Henry and Mudge
Under the Yellow Moon**
**Phonics:** Long Vowels *a, i*

# Long Vowels *a, i*

Write the words where they belong.  Then write four
more words of your own in each column.

```
···············  Word Bank  ···············
   grade      time      wide      gaze
   mile       crate     slide     blame
···········································
```

**a_e as in *skate***            **i_e as in *pride***

1. _____        9. _____

2. _____        10. _____

3. _____        11. _____

4. _____        12. _____

5. _____        13. _____

6. _____        14. _____

7. _____        15. _____

8. _____        16. _____

Name _____ Date _____

**Lesson 3**
PRACTICE BOOK

**Henry and Mudge
Under the Yellow Moon**
Introduce Comprehension:
Author's Purpose

# Author's Purpose

   Sam and Isabel were riding horses at camp.
Isabel's horse splashed across a small river.

   "Whoa!" said Isabel.

   "Don't be scared," said Sam.

   "I'm not scared," said Isabel.  "I'm wet."

   "That's why it is fun to ride a horse," said Sam.

   "Because you get wet?" asked Isabel.

   "No," said Sam.  "Because you never know what might
happen!  A horse can take you many places."

   "I like riding horses, but I like riding my bike in the city
more," said Isabel.  "A bike can take you places, too.  When I
ride a bike, I'm the one in charge.  And then I can stay dry!"

**Read the selection above.  Complete the Inference Map
below to show the author's purpose for writing this
selection.**

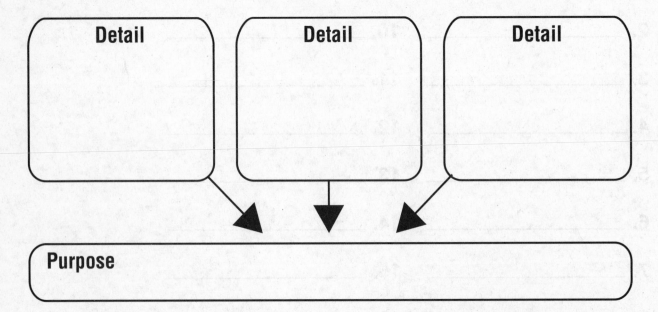

| Detail | Detail | Detail |
|---|---|---|

**Purpose**

# Long Vowels *a, i*

**Sort the Spelling Words by the long vowel sounds *a* and *i*.**

| Long *a* | Long *i* |
|---|---|
| 1. _____ | 8. _____ |
| 2. _____ | 9. _____ |
| 3. _____ | 10. _____ |
| 4. _____ | 11. _____ |
| 5. _____ | 12. _____ |
| 6. _____ | 13. _____ |
| 7. _____ | 14. _____ |

**Spelling Words**

**Basic Words**
1. cake
2. mine
3. plate
4. size
5. ate
6. grape
7. prize
8. wipe
9. race
10. line
11. pile
12. rake

**Review Words**
13. gave
14. bike

**Write the spelling pattern that answers each question.**

**15.** What spelling pattern do you see in words with the

long *a* sound? _____

**16.** What spelling pattern do you see in words with the

long *i* sound? _____

**Lesson 3**
PRACTICE BOOK

**Henry and Mudge
Under the Yellow Moon**
**Grammar:** Statements and
Questions

# Questions

> • A **question** begins with a **capital letter** and ends with a **question mark.**
>
> • Questions begin with question words: *who, what, when, where, how, why, is, are, does,* and *do.*
>
> <u>Do</u> you like dogs<u>?</u>

**Thinking Question**
*Does the sentence begin with a question word and end with a question mark?*

 **Write each question correctly.**

**1.** where will we walk.

_____

**2.** do you have a jacket

_____

**3.** who planted these trees

_____

**4.** is that a chipmunk.

_____

**5.** does your family like apple pie

_____

**6.** when will the sun go down

_____

# Focus Trait: Word Choice
# Sense Words

**Henry and Mudge
Under the Yellow Moon**
**Writing:** Write to Narrate

| Without Sense Words | Sense Words Added |
|---|---|
| I run across the grass. | I run across the <u>wet</u> grass and <u>feel the hot sun</u>. |

**Read each sentence below. Rewrite each sentence to include sense words.**

| Without Sense Words | Sense Words Added |
|---|---|
| **1.** <u>Outside my window there is a flag.</u> | _____ _____ |
| **2.** <u>The boy hits a baseball.</u> | _____ _____ |
| **3.** <u>The snow lies on the ground.</u> | _____ _____ |
| **4.** <u>The wind blows.</u> | _____ _____ |
| **5.** <u>We ate a good dinner.</u> | _____ _____ |

# Hard and Soft Sounds for *c*

**Complete the sentences about Cal and Cindy. Use words from the box.**

**Use words with the /k/ sound for *c* for Cal. Use words with the /s/ sound for *c* for Cindy.**

Word Bank

| cake | city |
| mice | rice |
| camp | cats |

**Cal**

**Cindy**

**1.** Cal has two pet

_____.

**4.** Cindy has two pet

_____.

**2.** Cal likes to eat

_____.

**5.** Cindy likes to eat

_____.

**3.** Cal went to a big

_____.

**6.** Cindy went to a big

_____.

Name _____ Date _____

**Lesson 3**
PRACTICE BOOK

**Henry and Mudge
Under the Yellow Moon**
Deepen Comprehension:
Author's Purpose

# Author's Purpose

Sara was walking home with her big sister, Amy.  Sara saw an old bird's nest.

"Why do birds make nests?" Sara asked.

"Birds make nests to keep their babies safe," Amy said.

"So a nest is like a house?" Sara asked.  "But it doesn't have a roof.  I don't like being wet when it rains."

"You wouldn't like eating bugs or worms, either," Amy laughed.  "Come on.  Let's go home."

"When we get home," Sara said, "I am going to say thank you to Mom."

"For keeping you safe when you were a baby?" Amy asked.

"For not feeding me bugs or worms."

They laughed and walked home together.

**Read the selection above.  Then use these questions and an Inference Map like the one here to identify the author's purpose for writing this selection.**

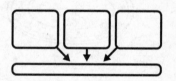

1. What reason does Sara give for wanting to thank her mom? _____

   _____

2. What details tell you this reason is a joke? _____

   _____

3. What does the author want to show you about Sara?

   _____

# Long Vowels *a, i*

**Write a Spelling Word for each picture.**

1. _____

4. _____

2. _____

5. _____

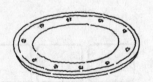

3. _____

6. _____

## Spelling Words

**Basic
Words**
1. cake
2. mine
3. plate
4. size
5. ate
6. grape
7. prize
8. wipe
9. race
10. line
11. pile
12. rake

**Review
Words**
13. gave
14. bike

**Write the Spelling Word that best completes each sentence.**

7. Jed won first place in the _____.

8. The mail is in a _____ on the table.

9. Is that your coat or _____?

10. I think I _____ too much pasta.

Name _____  Date _____

**Lesson 3**
PRACTICE BOOK

**Henry and Mudge
Under the Yellow Moon**
**Grammar:** Statements and Questions

# Statements and Questions

 **Write each statement correctly.**

**1.** The boy walks in the woods

_____

**2.** the dog runs beside the boy.

_____

**3.** they both have fun in the woods

_____

**4.** Soon it is time to go home

_____

 **Write each question correctly.**

**5.** What color are the leaves

_____

**6.** Does the dog bark at chipmunks

_____

**7.** Do you want to walk in the woods

_____

**8.** when would you like to go?

_____

**Lesson 3**
PRACTICE BOOK

**Henry and Mudge
Under the Yellow Moon**
**Vocabulary Strategies:**
Multiple-Meaning Words

# Multiple-Meaning Words

**Read both definitions of each word. Then read the sentence. Put a checkmark next to the definition that best matches the meaning of the underlined word.**

**1. pet 1** an animal kept at home ☐

    **2** stroke or pat gently ☐

Which do you think makes a better <u>pet</u>, a cat or a dog?

**2. pick 1** take something with your hands ☐

    **2** choose something or someone ☐

Joe will <u>pick</u> four people to be on his team.

**3. cool 1** cold ☐

    **2** neat and interesting ☐

The winter air was <u>cool</u> and windy.

**4. kid 1** a child or young person ☐

    **2** a young goat ☐

I have liked to read since I was a <u>kid</u>.

**5. raise 1** move or lift something higher ☐

    **2** make an amount or number bigger ☐

Mr. Jones goes outside to <u>raise</u> the flag at school each morning.

# Proofread for Spelling

**Proofread the story. Circle the six misspelled words.
Then write the correct spellings on the lines below.**

I was working in the yard when Jake and Ken
stopped by with a new byke.

"Is it yours?" I asked Ken.

"No," Jake said. "It's mien. Do you want to rase?"

"Yeah, let's!" I answered. I took my rak and made
a starting lyne in the dirt. "Ken, you be the judge and
give the winner a prise!"

## Spelling Words

**Basic Words**

1. cake
2. mine
3. plate
4. size
5. ate
6. grape
7. prize
8. wipe
9. race
10. line
11. pile
12. rake

1. _____   4. _____

2. _____   5. _____

3. _____   6. _____

**Change one letter in each word to make a Spelling Word.**

7. ripe _____   10. ape _____

8. slate _____   11. lake _____

9. side _____   12. tile _____

Name _____ Date _____

Lesson 3
PRACTICE BOOK

Henry and Mudge
Under the Yellow Moon
**Grammar:** Spiral Review

# Kinds of Adjectives

 **Circle the adjective in the sentence.**

**1.** We love our quiet woods.

**2.** The apples smell sweet.

**3.** He kicks the dry leaves.

**4.** I hear a noisy dog.

**Find the adjective in each sentence.  Write the adjective on the line.**

**5.** David has a small dog.

_____

**6.** I ate two apples.

_____

**7.** We ran in the cool breeze.

_____

**8.** I patted the friendly dog.

_____

**Grammar**

44

Grade 2, Unit 1: Neighborhood Visit

# Sentence Fluency

> **Statement:** Jan likes sweet apples.
>
> **Question:** Does Jan like sweet apples?
>
> **Question:** Is Dave walking his dog?
>
> **Statement:** Dave is happy walking his dog.

 **Change each sentence to another kind of sentence.
The word in ( ) tells what kind of sentence to write.**

**1.** Jan has fun climbing trees. (question)

_____

**2.** Do the children need coats? (statement)

_____

**3.** Dave feeds his dog. (question)

_____

**4.** Is Dave ready to pick apples? (statement)

_____

**5.** Jan wants to rake leaves. (question)

_____

**6.** Does Dave walk in the woods? (statement)

_____

Name _____  Date _____

# Long Vowels *o, u, e*

**Diary of a Spider**
Phonics: Long Vowels *o, u, e*

**Read the words in the box.  Cross out the words with short vowels.  Use the words that are left to complete the jokes.**

| | | |
|---|---|---|
| mole | home | stamp |
| Luke | blond | rust |
| hunt | Ken | mask |
| rose | stone | nose |
| nest | broke | |

What do you get if you toss a big s_____ into a little lake?

A wet stone!

What smells best at Jen's h_____?

Jen's n_____!

What did the m_____ say to the r_____?

Hi Bud!

What did L_____ say when he b_____ his leg in two spots?

I will never go back to those two spots!

# Nouns for People and Animals

A **noun** is a word that names a person or animal. A noun can name one or more than one.

A <u>spider</u> spins a web.

**Thinking Question**
*Which word names a person or animal?*

**Read each sentence. Write the noun that names a person or animal.**

**1.** The bee plays on the swings.

_____

**2.** The girls run away.

_____

**3.** An ant walks on the picnic blanket.

_____

**4.** The boy eats his lunch.

_____

**5.** The butterfly has a birthday.

_____

**6.** The leaf fell on two caterpillars.

_____

# Long Vowels *o, u, e*

Add *e* to finish each word.

Then use the words in the puzzle.

> **Word Bank**
>
> pol___   cub___   nos___   rul___
>
> rud___   tun___   ston___   smok___

**Across**

**2.** what to do or not do

**4.** rock

**5.** a flag is on it

**7.** can be made of ice

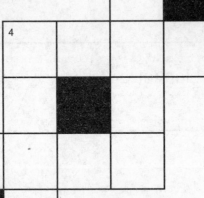

**Down**

**1.** sing it

**3.** smell with it

**4.** made when paper burns

**6.** not very nice

# Cause and Effect

I used to live alone on top of a huge hill. All day, all I did was blow fire and smoke on the people who lived at the bottom of the hill. So being a dragon was not much fun.

Then Ling came to visit. She walked up the huge hill. She ran through the smoke and the fire. She asked me to come to her birthday party!

Because I was so surprised, I started to cry. My tears made a river. The people at the bottom of the hill used my river to water the food they were growing.

I went to Ling's birthday party, too. I used my fire to light candles and keep people warm. The kids loved it!

Now I live with my friends at the bottom of the hill. Being a dragon is lots of fun now!

**Read the selection above. Complete the T-Map below to show the causes and effects in the selection.**

| **Cause** Why did it happen? | **Effect** What happened? |
|---|---|
| 1. | 1. |
| 2. | 2. |
| 3. | 3. |

# Long Vowels *o, u*

Sort the Spelling Words by the long vowel sounds *o* and *u*.

| Long *o* | Long *u* |
|---|---|
| 1. _____ | 13. _____ |
| 2. _____ | 14. _____ |
| 3. _____ | 15. _____ |
| 4. _____ | 16. _____ |
| 5. _____ | 17. _____ |
| 6. _____ | 18. _____ |
| 7. _____ | |
| 8. _____ | |
| 9. _____ | |
| 10. _____ | |
| 11. _____ | |
| 12. _____ | |

### Spelling Words

**Basic Words**
1. doze
2. nose
3. use
4. rose
5. pole
6. close
7. cute
8. woke
9. mule
10. rode
11. role
12. tune

**Review Words**
13. home
14. joke

Add two words you know with the long *o* sound to the
list. Then add two words you know with the long *u* sound.

# Nouns for Places and Things

- Not all nouns name people and animals.

- Nouns also name **places** and **things**.

Spider went to a <u>party</u>.

**Thinking Question**
*Which word names a place or thing?*

 **Write the noun that names the place or thing.**

**1.** Ladybug ate a cookie.

_____

**2.** Beetle baked a pie.

_____

**3.** Ant went to the store.

_____

**4.** Butterfly writes a song.

_____

**5.** The soup spilled on the bees.

_____

**6.** Fly loves a party.

_____

# Focus Trait: Ideas
# Main Idea

All of the sentences in a paragraph should be about the main idea. Below, the writer crossed out a sentence because it was not about the main idea.

**Main idea:** I went to the park with my sister today.

I went to the park with my sister today. We tried the seesaw. It didn't work. ~~Grampa says that in his day, flies and spiders did not get along.~~ We tried the tire swing. It didn't work, either.

**Read the main idea and the details below it. Cross out the detail sentence that does not tell more about the main idea.**

1. **Main idea:** I'm sleeping over at my friend's house.

   After dinner, we will watch a movie.

   We will stay up late.

   I forgot my homework today.

   We will tell scary stories.

2. **Main idea:** A big storm is coming this way.

   The wind is blowing things around.

   My friends like to swim in a pool.

   The sky is getting dark.

   Cold rain has already started.

# Hard and Soft Sounds for *g*

**Complete the sentences.  Use words from the box.**

> ### Word Bank
>
> garden      magic      dig       gave
> gate        huge       giant

**1.** Today Granny _____ me some

seeds.

**2.** Now we can start a _____ .

**3.** We start work next to the _____ .

**4.** We will _____ before we plant the seeds.

**5.** Granny says seeds are like _____ .

**6.** A little seed grows into a _____ plant.

**7.** I hope our plants grow as big as a _____ !

# Identify Cause and Effect

**Read the story below.**

I'm a big, hairy spider with many tiny eyes. I used to live in the East, but I wanted to move. People there would scream whenever they saw me!

So I came to the Southwest in a box of apples. The sun is always hot here, and the sand is soft. I take long naps. I use my long teeth to get things to eat.

I love to play with my friend Beetle. Sometimes we roll big balls across the sand. Then we bury them. I always forget where they are hidden, but Beetle finds them. When we play hide-and-go-seek, she finds me right away, too. Her strong nose makes it easy for her to smell things. She can use her nose to find them!

**Answer the questions. Then complete a T-Map to show other causes and effects from the story.**

| | |
|---|---|
| | |
| | |

**1.** Why would people scream whenever they saw this spider?

_____

_____

**2.** Beetle has a strong nose. What effect does this have on her life?

_____

Name _____ Date _____

# Long Vowels *o, u*

**Diary of a Spider**
Spelling: Long Vowels *o, u*

**Spelling Words**

**Basic Words**
1. doze
2. nose
3. use
4. rose
5. pole
6. close
7. cute
8. woke
9. mule
10. rode
11. role
12. tune

**Review Words**
13. home
14. joke

**Write the Spelling Word that belongs in each group.**

1. horse, donkey, _____

2. music, song, _____

3. daisy, sunflower, _____

4. actor, play, _____

5. ears, eyes, _____

6. house, apartment, _____

7. funny, laugh, _____

8. stick, rod, _____

9. sleep, nap, _____

**Read the word or words. Write the Spelling Word that means the opposite.**

10. throw away _____

11. open _____

12. slept _____

# Kinds of Nouns

 Write the noun that names a person or animal in each sentence.

**1.** The girl sees a web.

_____

**2.** The boy screams!

_____

**3.** The spider scurries away.

_____

**4.** The grass tickled the dog.

_____

 Write the noun that names a place or thing.

**5.** Spider carries a suitcase.

_____

**6.** Beetle puts on his hat.

_____

**7.** The snow fell on the bugs.

_____

**8.** The bugs move inside the garage.

_____

Name _____ Date _____

**Lesson 4**
PRACTICE BOOK

**Diary of a Spider**
**Vocabulary Strategies:**
Context Clues

# Context Clues

**Read the sentences. Use context clues to figure out the meaning of the underlined words. Circle the definition that best matches the meaning of the word.**

1. We <u>travel</u> to many countries. Sometimes we travel by plane. Sometimes we travel by ship.
   a. to eat
   b. to go on a trip
   c. to grow

2. I want to <u>learn</u> how to play the piano. A piano teacher can teach me to play.
   a. to get knowledge
   b. to read about something
   c. to see

3. Cats run away when dogs <u>scare</u> them.
   a. to yell loudly
   b. to jump or skip
   c. to make someone feel afraid

4. Julio <u>brought</u> his folder home in his backpack.
   a. forgot something
   b. carried something
   c. hid something

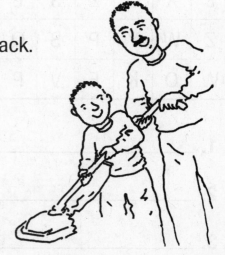

# Proofread for Spelling

**Diary of a Spider**
**Spelling:** Long Vowels *o, u*

**Proofread the announcement.  Cross out the four misspelled words. Then write them correctly in the margin.**

     Classmates!  Can you carry a toone?  Do you have a noze for talent?  Try out for a roll in this year's play.  We can youse you!

**Circle the six Spelling Words in the Word Search.  Then write the words below.**

| X | P | E | W | U | M | V | S | R |
|---|---|---|---|---|---|---|---|---|
| H | R | Q | A | C | U | T | E | O |
| C | L | O | S | E | L | V | D | S |
| E | X | U | Z | S | E | W | F | E |
| Z | W | Y | P | B | Q | F | R | J |
| W | O | K | E | V | P | O | L | E |

## Spelling Words

1. doze
2. nose
3. use
4. rose
5. pole
6. close
7. cute
8. woke
9. mule
10. rode
11. role
12. tune

## Review Words

13. home
14. joke

1. _____    4. _____

2. _____    5. _____

3. _____    6. _____

# Possessive Pronouns

  **Circle the correct pronoun to complete the sentence.**

**1.** The web is in (my, mine) tree.

**2.** Mom says the web is (my, hers).

**3.** She says the next bug on the web is (mine, your).

**4.** Come share (my, mine) tasty treat.

**Circle the pronoun that can take the place of each underlined word or group of words.**

**5.** I like <u>Spider's</u> web.

**his**                    **your**

**6.** It looks like <u>the web that belongs to me</u>.

**your**                    **mine**

**7.** I am <u>Beetle's</u> friend.

**my**                    **his**

**8.** I give food to <u>Ladybug</u>.

**my**                    **her**

# Word Choice

| Noun | Exact Noun |
|------|-----------|
| animal | spider |
| place | park |

**Replace each underlined word with an exact noun from the Word Box below.**

The spiders have a picnic. Every bug at the picnic brings some food. Beetle brings <u>food</u>. Caterpillar
1

brings <u>drink</u>. The party is near the <u>flowers</u>. The bugs
2                   3

all sing and dance. They have a great time. <u>Insect</u> must
4

leave early. Baby Bee has flying lessons. <u>Bird</u> is the
5

teacher.

| Crow | roses | Bee | pasta | juice |
|------|-------|-----|-------|-------|

1. _____

2. _____

3. _____

4. _____

5. _____

# Consonant Blends with *r, l, s*

**Read the words in the box.  Underline the blends.**
**Then use the words to complete Greta's letter.**

### Word Bank

| | | | |
|---|---|---|---|
| skate | best | cold | plane |
| Clare | stripes | smile | froze |

Dear _____,

    Soon I will be on a

_____ to your house.  I

_____ when I think of it!

How _____ is it there?  I

will bring my _____ mittens.

They have _____ on them.

I hope the pond _____!

Then we can _____ on it.

                Your friend,
                Greta

Name _____ Date _____

Lesson 5
PRACTICE BOOK

Teacher's Pets
Grammar: Singular and Plural
Nouns

# One and More Than One

- A **singular** noun names one person, animal, place, or thing.
- A **plural** noun names more than one person, animal, place, or thing.
- Add **-s** to most nouns to make them plural.

She has a <u>pet</u>.    Two <u>pets</u> play.

**Thinking Question**
*Does the noun name one or more than one?*

 **Decide if the underlined noun is singular or plural.**

**1.** Many <u>students</u> have pets.

    **singular**        **plural**

**2.** One <u>cat</u> purrs softly.

    **singular**        **plural**

**3.** Some <u>crickets</u> are noisy.

    **singular**        **plural**

**4.** A <u>hamster</u> is furry.

    **singular**        **plural**

**5.** Three <u>kittens</u> play happily.

    **singular**        **plural**

**6.** The <u>teacher</u> watches quietly.

    **singular**        **plural**

# Consonant Blends with *r, l, s*

Matt can't decide!  Help him by writing words from the box.

Compare your advice to a classmate's advice.

### Word Bank

| | | | |
|---|---|---|---|
| plums | milk | slides | sprint |
| frog | skate | snake | Wild West |
| swings | Space Trek | grin | brag |

**1.** What is the most fun to play on?

_____

_____

**2.** What is the best snack?

_____

_____

**3.** What is the best animal?

_____

_____

**4.** What is the best way to go around the block?

_____

_____

**5.** What should I do if I win something?

_____

_____

**6.** What would be the best trip?

_____

_____

Name _____  Date _____

**Lesson 5**
PRACTICE BOOK

**Teacher's Pets**
Introduce Comprehension:
Story Structure

# Story Structure

Everyone was talking about it!  Two whales had made a mistake.  They were swimming in the river and not in the ocean!

Maria and her dad went to the river to see the whales.  Hundreds of people were there.  Dad picked up Maria and put her above his head.  She looked at the river.

There they were!  The whales were swimming along, huge and shiny.  Then they were gone.

Dad smiled at Maria.  "How do you feel now?" he asked.

"Oh, Dad," said Maria.  "I am so glad I saw them!  And I am so glad they have made it home."

**Read the selection above.  Then complete the Story Map to show the parts of the story.**

| Characters | Setting |
|---|---|
| | |

**Plot**

**Beginning**

**Middle**

**End**

# Consonant Blends with *r*, *l*, *s*

Sort the Spelling Words by the consonant blends. One of the words belongs in two groups.

## Spelling Words

**Basic Words**

1. spin
2. clap
3. grade
4. swim
5. place
6. last
7. test
8. skin
9. drag
10. glide
11. just
12. stage

**Review Words**

13. slip
14. drive

**r Blends**

1. _____
2. _____
3. _____

**l Blends**

4. _____
5. _____
6. _____
7. _____

**s Blends**

8. _____
9. _____
10. _____
11. _____
12. _____
13. _____
14. _____
15. _____

**Write a Spelling Word that fits each sentence below.**

**16.** This Spelling Word has an *s* blend at the beginning.

_____

**17.** This Spelling Word has an *s* blend at the end.

_____

# Making Nouns Plural

- Use **plural** nouns when you are talking about more than one.
- Add -*s* to most nouns to name more than one.

| Singular | Plural |
|---|---|
| My <u>cat</u> drank milk. | My <u>cats</u> drank milk. |

**Thinking Question**
*Does the noun name one or more than one?*

 **Change the underlined noun into a plural noun.**

**Write the new sentence.**

**1.** The <u>pie</u> sat on the table.

_____

**2.** The <u>smell</u> filled the classroom.

_____

**3.** The <u>cat</u> jumped.

_____

**4.** The <u>plate</u> fell to the floor.

_____

**5.** The <u>girl</u> looked surprised.

_____

**6.** The <u>pet</u> ran away.

_____

# Focus Trait:
# Sentence Fluency
# Time-Order Words

| Time-Order Words |
| --- |
| first, then, last, soon, next, tomorrow, later, last night, today |

**Read each pair of sentences. Rewrite the sentences by adding the time-order word given.**

**1.** The puppy was tired. It sat down. (Then)

_____

**2.** It was getting dark outside. It would be time to go home. (Soon)

_____

_____

**3.** The puppy stood up. It ran home. (Next,)

_____

_____

**Write two sentences. Use at least one time-order word.**

**4.** _____

_____

**67**

# Cumulative Review

**Read the clues. Write the correct word on the line.**

gold
stove
slide
game
plane
scrape
flute
cage

**1.** It starts like **plan**.

It rhymes with **lane**.

It goes fast and high.

What is it?

_____

**2.** It starts like **slid**.

It rhymes with **side**.

You play on it.

What is it?

_____

**3.** It starts like **cat**.

It rhymes with **page**.

A pet bird can live in it.

What is it?

_____

**4.** It starts like **stop**.

It has a long **o** sound.

Dad makes dinner

with it.

What is it?

_____

**5.** It starts like **gas**.

It rhymes with **same**.

It is fun to play.

What is it?

_____

**6.** It starts like **flag**.

It rhymes with **cute**.

You play a tune on it.

What is it?

_____

Name _____     Date _____

**Lesson 5**
PRACTICE BOOK

**Teacher's Pets**
**Deepen Comprehension:**
Story Structure

# Story Structure

**Read the selection below.**

"I cannot find my pencils," Mr. Jones told his cat, Felix. "Yesterday, I couldn't find my pens."

Felix looked up from his pillow and yawned. Mr. Jones went to get his house key. It was not on the table!

He began to look for the key. He took the pillows off the sofa. He looked under his papers and in his piles of books. He checked his coat pockets and his old shoes. Nothing!

Finally, Mr. Jones said to Felix. "It's time to check you."

Felix leaped up and ran off. There, on Felix's pillow, sat five pencils, three pens, and a set of house keys.

**Answer the questions about story elements to retell the story.**

1. What is the setting and who are the characters in this story?

_____

2. Complete a Story Map by listing an event in the beginning, middle, and end. Retell the story.

_____

_____

_____

Name _____ Date _____

# Consonant Blends with *r, l, s*

Teacher's Pets
**Spelling:** Consonant Blends
with *r, l, s*

## Spelling Words

### Basic Words

1. spin
2. clap
3. grade
4. swim
5. place
6. last
7. test
8. skin
9. drag
10. glide
11. just
12. stage

### Review Words

13. slip
14. drive

**Write a Spelling Word for each clue.**

1. opposite of *first* _____

2. to go around fast _____

3. It covers your body. _____

4. to pull hard _____

5. to steer a car _____

6. to slide or fall _____

7. pat hands together _____

**Write the Spelling Word that makes sense.**

8. This word is used by actors. _____

9. This word rhymes with *rust.* _____

10. This word may be used when giving directions.

_____

11. This word is what you do when you ice skate. _____

12. This word is something a teacher might give you in

school. _____

# Singular and Plural Nouns

 **Write the sentences. Use the plural nouns.**

**1.** Two (rabbit, rabbits) run a race.

_____

**2.** The (turtle, turtles) join in.

_____

**3.** Many (student, students) laugh.

_____

**4.** The (pet, pets) run as fast as they can.

_____

 **Change the underlined noun into a plural noun.**
**Write the new sentence.**

**5.** The <u>bird</u> flew in the window.

_____

**6.** The <u>frog</u> jumped around the room.

_____

**7.** The <u>snake</u> hissed loudly.

_____

**8.** The <u>student</u> walked outside.

_____

# Word Endings -*ed*, -*ing*

**Choose the word that best completes each sentence.**
**Write the word on the line.**

**1.** Troy and Chad _____ to school yesterday.

**walked**                    **walking**

**2.** Vicky is _____ Tina on the phone now.

**called**                    **calling**

**3.** I see two dogs _____ at that cat.

**barked**                    **barking**

**4.** My grandma _____ with us last summer.

**stayed**                    **staying**

**5.** Yesterday the teacher _____ us a question.

**asked**                    **asking**

**6.** Dad took the key and _____ the gate.

**locked**                    **locking**

# Proofread for Spelling

**Proofread the paragraph.  Circle the six misspelled words.
Then write the words on the lines below.**

I like sports.  I like to swimm, but my favorite sport
is ice skating.  My sister is a great skater.  I juhst like
to watch her glid around the ice.  She is so good that
people clapp when she skates.  The ice is her stagge.  If I
had to give her a graide, it would be an *A.*

1. _____   4. _____

2. _____   5. _____

3. _____   6. _____

**Make a word chain by adding to the words below.  Use as
many Spelling Words as you can.**

```
          S
          T
          A
  G R A D E
          E
```

## Spelling Words

**Basic
Words**
1. spin
2. clap
3. grade
4. swim
5. place
6. last
7. test
8. skin
9. drag
10. glide
11. just
12. stage

**Review
Words**
13. slip
14. drive

# Adjectives That Compare

✏️   **Circle the adjective that makes each sentence correct.**

**1.** Our pet is (loud, louder) than yours.

**2.** A lizard is the (quieter, quietest) of all pets.

**3.** Your rabbit jumps (high, higher) than my dog.

**4.** A frog jumps the (higher, highest) of all the animals.

**5.** Our class pet is the (greater, greatest) pet in the school.

✏️   **Use adjectives from the box to finish each sentence.**
**Write the adjective on the line.**

| slow | slower | slowest |
|------|--------|---------|

**6.** Our classroom pet is very _____.

**7.** The snail is the _____ pet of all.

**8.** The snail is _____ than the turtle.

# Conventions

| Singular Nouns | Plural Nouns |
|---|---|
| one lizard | two lizards |
| a student | many students |

**Rewrite each sentence. Use the plural for each underlined noun.**

**1.** We saw many <u>pet</u> at school.

_____

**2.** Two <u>rabbit</u> lived with the first graders.

_____

**3.** Some <u>duck</u> quacked in the second grade class.

_____

**4.** Three <u>snake</u> hissed in the third grade class.

_____

**5.** The fourth graders fed some <u>spider</u>.

_____

**6.** Many <u>animal</u> lived at the school.

_____

# Common Final Blends
## *nd, ng, nk, nt, ft, xt, mp*

**Write the name of each picture. Then circle the final consonant blend.**

1. _____

2. _____

3. _____

4. _____

5. _____

6. _____

7. _____

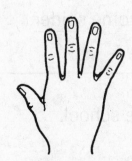

8. _____

9. _____

Grade 2, Unit 2: Nature Watch

# Adding *-es* to Nouns

- Add *-s* to most nouns to **name more than one.**
- Add *-es* to nouns that end with *s, x, ch,* and *sh* to **name more than one.**

one fox      two foxes

Two (fox, <u>foxes</u>) live in a den.

**Thinking Question**
*Do I need a noun that names one or a noun that names more than one?*

Write the correct noun in each sentence. Reread each sentence to make sure that the noun makes sense.

**1.** The fox den is next to a _____.

(bush, bushes)

**2.** Mama Fox wears her _____.

(glass, glasses)

**3.** She makes three _____.

(lunch, lunches)

**4.** Papa Fox eats one _____.

(sandwich, sandwiches)

**5.** Baby Fox eats two _____.

(peach, peaches)

# Common Final Blends
# nd, ng, nk, nt, ft, xt, mp

**Answer each pair of clues using the words below them.**

**1.** Coming after: _____

Went away: _____

**next**                          **left**

**2.** A small lake: _____

To be on your feet: _____

**stand**                        **pond**

**3.** To take a sip: _____

Sleep in a tent: _____

**camp**                         **drink**

**4.** Write letters on a page: _____

Look for something that is lost: _____

**print**                        **hunt**

**5.** A tune you can sing: _____

The sound a horn makes: _____

**honk**                         **song**

# Text and Graphic Features

### The Barn Owl

The barn owl is a brown bird with a white face. Its face is shaped like a heart. Its beak is white-yellow, the same color as **ivory**. An owl has feathers on its legs.

### Hunting for Food

The barn owl hunts alone at night. Its **prey** are small animals such as mice. It can see and hear the smallest movement. Its wings are almost **silent**. The mouse cannot hear it coming. The barn owl gets the mouse and flies off.

### Finding a Home

Long ago, the barn owl lived in barns on farms. It would eat mice that lived in the barn. Today, the barn owl makes its home in buildings or hollow trees close to fields and forests.

**Read the selection above. Complete the T-Map by using text features to answer the questions about what you read.**

| | |
|---|---|
| **1.** What color is **ivory**? | **1.** |
| **2.** What is **prey**? What is the barn owl's prey? | **2.** |
| **3.** Where does the barn owl live today? | **3.** |

**Animals Building Homes**
Spelling: Common Final Blends
*nd, ng, nk, nt, ft, xt, mp*

# Final Blends *nd, ng, nk, nt, ft, xt, mp*

**Sort the Spelling Words by their final blends.**

*nd* blends  _____

*ng* blends  _____

*nk* blends  _____

*nt* blends  _____

*ft* blends  _____

*xt* blends  _____

*mp* blends  _____

**Now add two words that you know to any of the lists.**

## Spelling Words

**Basic Words**
1. next
2. end
3. camp
4. sank
5. sing
6. drink
7. hunt
8. stand
9. long
10. stamp
11. pond
12. bring

**Review Words**
13. jump
14. left

# Nouns That Change Spelling

Some nouns change their spelling to name more than one.

one child     two children

Two (child, <u>children</u>) find a nest.

**Thinking Question**
*Do I need a noun that names one or a noun that names more than one?*

✏ **Write the correct noun to finish each sentence.  Reread each sentence to make sure that it makes sense.**

1. Two _____ take a walk.

   (child, children)

2. They sit on a _____ in the park.

   (bench, benches)

3. One _____ sees a rabbit hole.

   (child, children)

4. Many _____ stand near the

   hole. (man, men)

5. Two _____ point to the hole.

   (woman, women)

# Focus Trait: Ideas
# Main Idea and Supporting Details

| Main Idea | Supporting Details |
|---|---|
| Why animals need homes | Keep them safe from enemies |
| | Protect them from weather |
| | Help them raise babies |

**Read each set of sentences. Underline the sentence that contains the main idea.**

1. Snakes also live in holes.

   Rabbits live underground in warrens.

   Many kinds of animals live in holes.

2. Some people live in apartments.

   People live in different kinds of houses.

   Some people live in ice houses called igloos.

3. They can protect you from harm.

   Dogs make good pets.

   They are loyal.

4. Some mammals live in the water.

   Dolphins look like fish, but they are mammals.

   Sea otters are mammals that live in the Pacific
   Ocean.

**82**

Name _____  Date _____

# Cumulative Review

**Read the words in the box.  Write the word that completes each sentence.**

### Word Bank

| nest | twigs | end |
|------|-------|-----|
| spring | play | branches |

1. The _____ of winter is near.

2. It is a sunny day in the _____.

3. Squirrels run and _____.

4. Buds on the _____ will open soon.

5. Two robins build a _____ in the tree.

6. They use _____ and grass to make it strong.

**On the lines below, write a word that begins with the beginning blends shown.**

7. br _____  9. fr _____  11. st _____

8. pr _____  10. cl _____  12. tr _____

# Text and Graphic Features

**Read the selection below.**

## The Strange Life of the Koala

The koala looks like a bear because it is small and furry. But it is not a bear. It is a **marsupial**, like a kangaroo.

### Shelter

You won't find koalas in nests or burrows. They spend their lives at the top of **eucalyptus** trees. These trees grow up to 400 feet tall. Koalas sit on high branches and stay safe from **predators** down below.

### Diet

Koalas eat only one thing—eucalyptus leaves. An adult koala eats from 1 to 2 pounds of leaves in a day. The koala does not need to drink water. It gets all it needs from the leaves.

**Use text and graphic features to answer the questions. Complete a T-Map and write your answers on a separate sheet of paper.**

1. Based on the headings, what can you predict you will learn about?

2. Review the words in boldface print. Why do you think they are in bold?

**Lesson 6**
PRACTICE BOOK

# Final Blends *nd, ng, nk, nt, ft, xt, mp*

**Animals Building Homes**
Spelling: Common Final Blends
*nd, ng, nk, nt, ft, xt, mp*

## Spelling Words

**Use the Spelling Words to complete the story.**

My dad and I like to (1) _____ out. This year, Dad let me (2) _____ my friend Jason. It was a (3) _____ drive. Dad stopped near a clear (4) _____.

We don't (5) _____ animals, but we do like to fish. It was hot, so we brought a lot of water to (6) _____. Dad taught us to (7) _____ old songs. We had a great time! At the (8) _____ of the weekend, we didn't want to go home. Jason and I hope to go again (9) _____ year.

**Use the Spelling Words to fill in the blanks.**

**10.** Instead of sitting, you should _____.

**11.** I need a _____ to mail my letter.

**12.** The ship _____.

### Basic Words

1. next
2. end
3. camp
4. sank
5. sing
6. drink
7. hunt
8. stand
9. long
10. stamp
11. pond
12. bring

**Lesson 6**
PRACTICE BOOK

# More Nouns That Change Spelling

**Animals Building Homes**
**Grammar:** More Plural Nouns

> **Write the correct noun to finish each sentence.**
**Read the sentences to make sure that they make sense.**

1. Most men and _____ don't like to

see mice in their homes. (woman, women)

2. _____ work hard to build nests.

(Mouse, Mice)

3. They carry grass with their _____

_____. (tooth, teeth)

4. They pat down mud with their _____

_____. (foot, feet)

5. Many _____ can live in one

nest. (mice, mouse)

6. Most _____ like to look at nests.

(child, children)

# Prefixes *un-* and *re-*

**Choose the word from the box that best completes each sentence. Write the word on the line.**

Word Bank

| | | | |
|---|---|---|---|
| rehang | untie | rebuild | unreal |
| unfold | remake | unload | |

1. I _____ my shoes before I take them off.

2. Please _____ the blanket and put it on the bed.

3. I know that story is true, but it is so strange that it seems _____!

4. The picture fell off the wall, so I have to _____ it.

5. My little brother messed up my bed, so I had to _____ it.

6. The birds used twigs to _____ their nest after it fell out of the tree.

7. I helped Mom _____ all the food from the car.

# Proofread for Spelling

**Proofread the story. Circle the six misspelled words.
Then write the correct spellings on the lines below.**

I needed to buy a stampe to mail my letter. I was
at the end of a log line at the post office. One person
in line started to sang. Another took a drenk from a
water bottle. A grandpa tugged at a child and scolded,
"Stad still!" I was about to give up and go home when I
heard, "Nextt!" The line was finally moving.

## Spelling Words

### Basic Words

1. next
2. end
3. camp
4. sank
5. sing
6. drink
7. hunt
8. stand
9. long
10. stamp
11. pond
12. bring

1. _____    4. _____

2. _____    5. _____

3. _____    6. _____

**Write in the letters to spell the Basic Words.**

7. bri + ___ ___          9. ca + ___ ___

8. po + ___ ___          10. sa + ___ ___

# Parts of a Sentence

✏ **Read each sentence. The action part has one line underneath it. Draw two lines under the naming part.**

**1.** The cat and dog <u>live</u> in the house.

**2.** The puppy and kitten <u>play</u> together.

**3.** A man and woman <u>feed</u> them.

**4.** A boy and girl <u>pet</u> them.

**5.** An aunt and uncle <u>visit</u>.

✏ **Read each sentence. The naming part has two lines underneath it. Draw one line under the action part.**

**6.** <u>Tigers and bears</u> sleep in caves.

**7.** <u>Turtles and snails</u> live in shells.

**8.** <u>Bees and wasps</u> make hives.

**9.** <u>Birds and mice</u> build nests.

**10.** <u>Gophers</u> dig burrows.

# Sentence Fluency

| Short Sentences | New Sentence with Joined Subjects |
|---|---|
| Foxes live in dens.<br>Bears live in dens. | Foxes and bears live in dens. |

| Short Sentences | New Sentence with Joined Subjects |
|---|---|
| Mice make their own nests.<br>Birds make their own nests. | Mice and birds make their own nests. |

**Read the sentences below.  Use *and* to combine their subjects.  Write the new sentence on the line.**

1. Geese fly to warm places in winter.
   Ducks fly to warm places in winter.

   _____

2. Seals live in cold places.
   Penguins live in cold places.

   _____

3. Squirrels use the branches of trees.
   Crows use the branches of trees.

   _____

4. Baby finches are fed in nests.
   Baby cardinals are fed in nests.

   _____

**Lesson 7**
PRACTICE BOOK

# Double Consonants and *ck*

**The Ugly Vegetables**
**Phonics:** Double Consonants
and *ck*

**Read the words below. Think about how the words in each group are alike. Write the missing word that fits in each group.**

Word Bank

| quack | fluff | dress | duck |
|-------|-------|-------|------|
| mitt  | kick  | spill | neck |

**1.** pants, shirt, _____

**2.** fish, frog, _____

**3.** bat, ball, _____

**4.** arm, leg, _____

**5.** tip, splash, _____

**6.** moo, meow, _____

**7.** fur, fuzz, _____

**8.** run, jump, _____

**Write a word that rhymes with each word below.**

**9.** stall _____    **11.** back _____

**10.** mess _____    **12.** will _____

# Names for People and Animals

> Some **nouns** name special people or animals. These special nouns are **proper nouns**. Proper nouns begin with capital letters.
>
> Today <u>Lanie Lin</u> plants a garden.

**Thinking Question**
*Which word names a special person or animal?*

 **Write the proper nouns correctly.**

**1.** She gets help from maggie.

_____

**2.** Her cat whiskers looks on.

_____

**3.** They plant peas for eric barker.

_____

**4.** They plant tomatoes for peter andrews.

_____

**5.** They plant carrots for their rabbit hoppy.

_____

**The Ugly Vegetables**
Phonics: Double Consonants
and *ck*

# Double Consonants and *ck*

**Put these letters together to write words that end with double consonants.**

**1.** m + i + t + t = _____

**2.** g + l + a + s + s = _____

**3.** s + t + u + f + f = _____

**4.** b + e + l + l = _____

**5.** a + d + d = _____     | 2 + 2 = 4 |

**Now use the words you made above to complete the sentences below.**

**6.** I will fill my _____ with milk.

**7.** The _____ rings for class to start.

**8.** Pam wants to _____ all her
things into one bag.

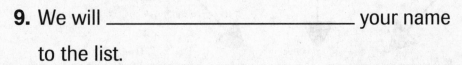

**9.** We will _____ your name
to the list.

**10.** Get your bat and _____.

# Conclusions

"I don't like cauliflower, Mom," Margie said. "Can we have mashed potatoes?"

"Hmmm," said Mom. "Maybe we can."

Margie went to her room. Mom cut the cauliflower up and cooked it to make it very soft. Then she mashed it all up. It was beginning to look like mashed potatoes!

Mom put in butter, pepper, and cheese.

Margie came to the table. "These mashed potatoes are a little different," said Mom. "I hope you like them!"

"Yum!" said Margie, taking a big bite. "These taste so good! You should make them more often!"

"Hmmm," smiled Mom.

**Read the story above. Complete an Inference Map to draw a conclusion about how Mom will make cauliflower next time.**

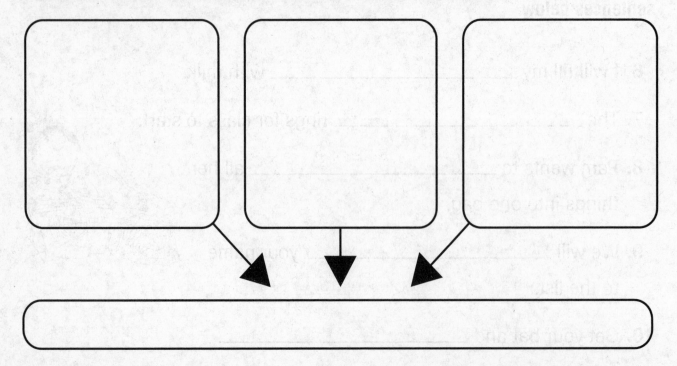

**Lesson 7**
PRACTICE BOOK

# Double Consonants and *ck*

**The Ugly Vegetables**
Spelling: Double Consonants
and *ck*

Sort the Spelling Words. Put words that end in *ck* in one list.
Put words that end in double consonants in the other list.

**Spelling Words**

### *ck* Words

1. _____

2. _____

3. _____

4. _____

5. _____

6. _____

7. _____

### Double Consonant Words

8. _____

9. _____

10. _____

11. _____

12. _____

13. _____

14. _____

15. _____

16. _____

**Basic
Words**

1. dress
2. spell
3. class
4. full
5. add
6. neck
7. stuck
8. kick
9. rock
10. black
11. trick
12. doll

**Review
Words**

13. will
14. off

**Add one more word that you know to each list.**

# Names for Places

**The Ugly Vegetables**
Grammar: Proper Nouns

Some **nouns** name special places, such as a street, city, state, or country.  These are also **proper nouns**.  Names for places begin with capital letters.

We just moved to <u>Atlanta</u>.

**Thinking Question**
*Which word names a special place?*

✎ **Rewrite each sentence. Write the name for each special place correctly.**

**1.** He has a garden on main street.

_____

**2.** It is the best garden in macon.

_____

**3.** People visit from all over georgia.

_____

**4.** Many visitors come from alabama.

_____

**5.** Cars can park on bell avenue.

_____

# Focus Trait: Organization
# Retelling Events in Order

| Events Not in Order | Events in Order |
|---|---|
| I woke up. <br> I brushed my teeth. <br> I put toothpaste on my toothbrush. | **1.** I woke up. <br> **2.** I put toothpaste on my toothbrush. <br> **3.** I brushed my teeth. |

**Work with a partner. Number each set of sentences in the order that makes the most sense.**

**1.** ___ I put on my shoes.

___ I put on my socks.

___ I tied my shoes.

**2.** ___ I had dinner.

___ I had breakfast.

___ I had lunch.

**Work on your own. Number each set of sentences in an order that makes sense.**

**3.** ___ The plants started to grow.

___ We planted seeds.

___ We dug up the soil.

**5.** ___ I went to school.

___ I woke up.

___ I grabbed my lunch.

**4.** ___ I took out a glass.

___ I poured milk.

___ I drank the milk.

# Double Consonants (CVC)

**Write a word from the box to complete each sentence below.**

> Word Bank
>
> happen    bottom    button    cotton    puppet

1. The dress is made of _____.

2. What will _____ if it starts to rain?

3. The children had fun at the _____ show.

4. The rag doll has a _____ for a nose.

5. The prize is at the _____ of the sack.

**Answer each clue using a word from the box.**

> Word Bank
>
> rabbit    kitten    hidden    mitten    muffin

6. Something good to eat _____

7. Another name for a bunny _____

8. It keeps your hand warm. _____

9. A baby cat _____

10. Hard to find _____

# Conclusions

**Read the selection below.**

### Winter Tomatoes

I love the tomatoes we grow in the summer. I told Mom I wanted to grow them in the winter. She helped me start a winter tomato garden.

We planted seeds in small pots. Soon little green shoots poked up. When the seedlings were three weeks old, Mom and I put them in bigger pots. I set the pots in a sunny corner of the barn. Then I made sure the plants got enough water and sunlight.

Soon there were little green tomatoes. They turned orange, and then red.

I ran to the road and posted a sign: "Tomatoes for Sale." People lined up to buy them! When Mom saw how much money we made, she smiled.

**Draw a conclusion to answer the question. Complete an Inference Map on a separate sheet of paper.**

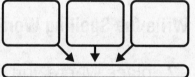

Where do you think the narrator lives? Find clues in the text to support your answer.

_____

_____

_____

_____

# Double Consonants and *ck*

**The Ugly Vegetables**
Spelling: Double Consonants
and *ck*

**Write the Spelling Word for each picture.**

$2 + 2$

1. _____    4. _____

2. _____    5. _____

3. _____    6. _____

**Write the Spelling Word that matches each clue.**

7. place where you go to school     _____

8. to get trapped     _____

9. something you do with your foot     _____

10. something you do with words     _____

11. when you cannot put in more     _____

12. a toy that looks like a baby     _____

# Writing Proper Nouns

✏️ **Rewrite each sentence. Write the name for each special person or animal correctly.**

**1.** My friend mark visits my garden.

_____

**2.** I give christine clark sunflowers.

_____

**3.** I give water to our dog spotty.

_____

✏️ **Rewrite each sentence. Write the name for each special place correctly.**

**4.** Grapes grow on franklin road.

_____

**5.** Olives grow in italy.

_____

**6.** Apples grow in portland.

_____

# Homophones

**Word Bank**

| too | won | wear | plain |
|-----|-----|------|-------|
| two | one | where | plane |

**Choose the word from the box that best completes the sentence. Write the word on the line.**

**1.** The farmer has _____ shovels.

**2.** _____ did you put my keys?

**3.** I don't like stripes or spots. I only like to wear _____ clothes.

**4.** I am happy because my team _____ the game.

**5.** My sister is going to the movies. I want to go, _____!

**6.** I have only _____ flower in the vase.

**7.** What are you going to _____ to the party?

**8.** We will take a car to the airport, and then we will get on a _____.

# Proofread for Spelling

**Proofread the journal entry. Circle the five misspelled words. Then spell the words correctly on the lines below.**

Today we went on a clas trip. The first bus was ful, so we waited for the next one. After about a block, the bus ran over a big rouck. There was a loud noise and then the bus stopped. The driver said that we were stukk. He had to ad air to the tire before we could go.

| Spelling Words |
| --- |
| **Basic Words** |
| 1. dress |
| 2. spell |
| 3. class |
| 4. full |
| 5. add |
| 6. neck |
| 7. stuck |
| 8. kick |
| 9. rock |
| 10. black |
| 11. trick |
| 12. doll |

1. _____

2. _____

3. _____

4. _____

5. _____

**Unscramble the letters in each Spelling Word.**

6. olld _____

7. cablk _____

8. ustck _____

9. eknc _____

10. kkic _____

11. lwil _____

12. elpsl _____

# Complete Sentences

✎ Add a naming part or action part to each word group to make a complete sentence. Write the new sentence.

**1.** likes to grow pumpkins

_____

**2.** the farmer

_____

**3.** plants many tomatoes

_____

✎ Draw one line under each sentence that shows the correct word order.

**4.** John grows carrots.

Grows carrots John.

**5.** Lori needs more seeds.

More seeds Lori needs.

**6.** Beans she wants to plant.

She wants to plant beans.

**104**

# Word Choice

| Sentence Without Exact Nouns | Sentence With Exact Nouns |
|---|---|
| A man plants cherry trees along a street. | Jim Brown plants cherry trees along Sweet Street. |

**Read the paragraph. Replace the underlined words with exact words from the word box. Write the exact words on the lines below.**

| | | |
|---|---|---|
| Carol Ach | Ohio | Columbus |
| Sparky | Jack | |

A woman has a big garden.  She grows the best lettuce and tomatoes in the state.  Her son, Jack, helps. Every summer, people come from the city to her farm stand.  The son sets everything up.  His dog, Sparky, looks on.  The dog wags his tail every time a new customer comes by.

**1.** A woman _____

**2.** the state _____

**3.** the city _____

**4.** The son _____

**5.** The dog _____

**Lesson 8**
PRACTICE BOOK

**Super Storms**
Phonics: Consonant Digraphs
*th, sh, wh, ch, tch, ph*

# Words with *th, sh, wh, ch, tch, ph*

**Write a word from the box to answer each riddle.**

### Word Bank

| | | | | |
|---|---|---|---|---|
| math | white | fish | bath | ship |
| watch | chick | phone | dish | wheel |

**1.** It can swim. It has a big fin. It is a _____.

**2.** It is a class in school. It uses numbers. It is

_____.

**3.** It comes from an egg. It has soft fluff. It is a

_____.

**4.** It has two hands. It tells you the time. It is a

_____.

**5.** It floats in the sea. Many people ride on it. It is a

_____.

**6.** It is on a car. It helps the car move. It is a

_____.

**7.** It can ring. You use it to chat with a pal. It is a

_____.

# Action Verbs

A **verb** names an action that someone or something does or did.

The wind <u>blows</u> hard.

**Thinking Question**
*Which word names an action?*

Read each sentence. **Underline the verb in each sentence.**

1. The clouds cover the sky.

2. The rain pours down.

3. People run for cover.

4. Water flows in the street.

5. The sun shines.

6. The children play.

7. Children splash in puddles.

8. It rains again after supper.

9. This time everyone stays dry.

10. Everyone sits inside.

Name _____ Date _____

**Super Storms**
**Phonics:** Consonant Digraphs
*th, sh, wh, ch, tch, ph*

# Words with *th, sh, wh, ch, tch, ph*

**Put these letters together to write words with *th, sh,
wh, ch, tch,* or *ph*. Then read each word.**

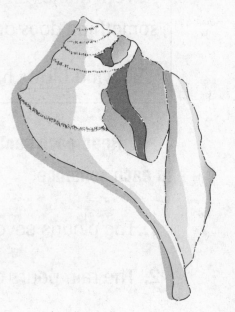

**1.** c + h + i + p = _____

**2.** s + h + e + l + l = _____

**3.** g + r + a + p + h = _____

**4.** t + h + i + n = _____

**5.** w + i + s + h = _____

**6.** w + h + i + t + e = _____

**7.** m + a + t + c + h = _____

**8.** p + a + t + h = _____

**Write a word you know that begins with each pair of letters.**

**9.** ch _____ **11.** sh _____

**10.** th _____ **12.** ph _____

# Main Ideas and Details

When a hurricane is born, scientists need to study it right away. To do this, they call in the Hurricane Hunters.

Hurricane Hunters are a group of pilots. They fly right into hurricanes! They get the facts. They find out how big the hurricane is, how strong it is, and where it is going. They send the facts by radio to people on the ground.

Hurricane Hunters need to be brave. When they fly close to the eye of a hurricane, the ride gets very bumpy! Clouds and rain also make it hard to see. Sometimes Hurricane Hunters can't even see the wings on their plane!

Hurricane Hunters are important. They help people on the ground know what to do when a hurricane is coming.

**Read the article above. Complete the Web below to show two details that support the main idea of the third paragraph.**

DETAIL:

DETAIL:

MAIN IDEA: Hurricane Hunters need to be brave.

# Spelling Word Sort

**Super Storms**
**Spelling:** Consonant Digraphs *th, sh, wh, ch, tch*

Sort the Spelling Words under the headings below. If a word can sort into more than one place, choose one.

| *th* | *sh* | *wh* |
|------|------|------|
| _____ | _____ | _____ |
| _____ | _____ | _____ |
| _____ | _____ | _____ |
| _____ | _____ | |

*ch*

_____

_____

_____

**Think about the letters *th, sh, wh,* and *ch*. Which**
**Spelling Word could go under two of the headings above?**

_____

| Spelling Words |
|---|
| **Basic Words** |
| 1. dish |
| 2. than |
| 3. chest |
| 4. such |
| 5. thin |
| 6. push |
| 7. shine |
| 8. chase |
| 9. white |
| 10. while |
| 11. these |
| 12. flash |
| **Review Words** |
| 13. which |
| 14. then |

# Action Verbs and Subjects

> A **verb** tells what someone or something does or did. The **subject** tells who or what is doing the action.
>
> The hail <u>pounds</u> on the roof.

**Thinking Question**
*Which word names an action? Who does or did the action?*

 **Read each sentence. The verb is underlined. Circle the subject.**

1. Jan <u>hears</u> the sounds.

2. The cat <u>hides</u> under the bed.

3. The hail <u>bounces</u> on the ground.

4. The clouds <u>turn</u> gray.

 **Read each sentence. The subject is circled. Underline the verb.**

5. The (air) gets cold.

6. (Ian) feels the rain.

7. The (dog) runs through puddles.

8. The (mail) stays dry.

# Focus Trait: Voice
# Using Your Own Words

**Read each sentence. For each underlined word or phrase,**
**circle another word that can take its place.**

**1.** While we were driving, it started to rain. The rain be-
  came a <u>violent</u> thunderstorm.

  **dangerous**          **silly**          **calm**

**2.** Our car was <u>tossed</u> back and forth by the winds.

  **fed**                **blown**          **held**

**3.** A traffic jam <u>stretched for</u> ten miles.

  **covered**            **dance**          **walk**

**Pair/Share** Work with a partner to rewrite each sentence in your
own words.

**4.** The moving and changing air makes thunderstorms
  happen.

  _____

**5.** Some thunderstorms become extremely strong, and
  then they can cause tornadoes.

  _____

  _____

# Base Words and Endings -s, -ed, -ing

**Read each word pair. Use the words to answer the clues.**

**1. prints          jumps**

Hops up and down          _____

Writes words on paper          _____

**2. lifting          camping**

Pulling something up          _____

Living outside and sleeping in a tent          _____

**3. packed          checked**

Looked at something again to be sure          _____

Put things in a box or a bag          _____

**4. passing          helping**

Doing part of the work          _____

Walking by a person or place          _____

**5. rested          hunted**

Took a nap          _____

Looked for something          _____

# Infer Main Ideas and Details

**Read the selection below.**

Long ago, people didn't have the tools we do today to find out about the weather. So they looked for signs in nature.

People saw that some plants changed when it was about to rain. Some flowers closed up when rain was on the way. They opened when the weather was nice. Pinecones did the same. They also closed up when rain was coming and opened when the weather was nice. Today scientists agree that these plants do predict rain!

Farmers long ago would also watch cows. Sometimes cows would sit down if rain was on the way. Today scientists say that cows predict rain only about half the time.

**Infer the main ideas and supporting details. Complete a Web and write your answers on a separate piece of paper.**

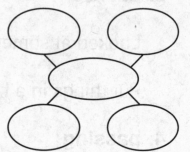

**1.** What is the main idea of this selection?

**2.** What are the supporting details of this selection?

# Words with *th, sh, wh, ch, tch*

**Super Storms**
Spelling: Consonant Digraphs *th, sh, wh, ch, tch*

**Write the Spelling Word that is the opposite of each word.**

**1.** dark _____

**2.** black _____

**3.** fat _____

**4.** now _____

**5.** pull _____

**6.** dull _____

**Complete each Spelling Word with a consonant digraph.**

**7.** di __ __

**8.** su __ __

**9.** __ __ est

**10.** __ __ an

**11.** __ __ ile

**12.** __ __ ase

**13.** __ __ ese

**14.** __ __ i __ __

## Spelling Words

**Basic Words**
1. dish
2. than
3. chest
4. such
5. thin
6. push
7. shine
8. chase
9. white
10. while
11. these
12. flash

**Review Words**
13. which
14. then

# Action Verbs

 **Read each sentence.  Underline the verb.**

**1.** The wind ended.

**2.** The thunder started.

**3.** We cover our ears.

**4.** We sit in the house

 **Read each sentence.  The action verb is underlined.**
**Circle the subject that is doing the action.**

**5.** Jerry <u>peeks</u> out the window.

**6.** The rain <u>floods</u> the street.

**7.** The water <u>flows</u> down the hill.

**8.** The storm <u>stops</u> the next day.

**116**

# Compound Words

Choose the word from the box that completes the compound word in each sentence.  Write the word on the line.

**Word Bank**

| light | time | fly | house |
|-------|------|-----|-------|
| writing | shine | book | print |

1. We built a dog + _____ for our new puppy to live in.

2. I have a flash + _____ in case it gets dark.

3. Please use neat hand + _____ when you do your homework.

4. Dee saw an orange butter + _____ fluttering in the garden.

5. Mark read his favorite story + _____ before bed.

6. Please don't touch the window with dirty hands. You'll leave a thumb + _____.

7. I can go out and play in the sun + _____.

8. In the summer + _____ we like to go to the pool.

# Proofread for Spelling

**Super Storms**
Spelling: Consonant Digraphs *th,
sh, wh, ch*

**Proofread the note. Circle the six misspelled words.
Then write the correct spellings on the lines below.**

Dear Mom,

    I want you to know that I broke the whitte dishe.

I am sorry.  Whil I was trying to pulsh the door of the

chast closed, it slipped out of my hands.  Spike was

covered in mud, and I was in a hurry to chese him

outside.  I will help you pay for a new dish.

       Love,

       Matt

| Spelling Words |
|---|
| **Basic Words** |
| 1. dish |
| 2. than |
| 3. chest |
| 4. such |
| 5. thin |
| 6. push |
| 7. shine |
| 8. chase |
| 9. white |
| 10. while |
| 11. these |
| 12. flash |

1. _____     4. _____

2. _____     5. _____

3. _____     6. _____

**Unscramble the letters to make a Spelling Word.**

7. cshu _____     10. shfla _____

8. ehtes _____     11. inshe _____

9. htna _____     12. nthi _____

# Statements and Questions

🖉 **Read each sentence. Circle the kind of sentence it is. Then rewrite the sentence correctly.**

**1.** will it rain today          statement          question

_____

**2.** i think it will snow          statement          question

_____

**3.** did you see the clouds          statement          question

_____

🖉 **Read the paragraph below. Then rewrite the paragraph correctly. Use question marks at the end of questions. Use periods at the end of statements. Remember to use capital letters.**

A storm hits our town  we stay in the house.  What else can we do.  mom gives us popcorn  Dad reads to us When will the storm end

_____

_____

_____

_____

# Word Choice

| Sentence without Exact Verbs | Sentence with Exact Verbs |
|---|---|
| The wind <u>blew</u> on the door. | The wind <u>slammed</u> on the door. |

| Sentence without Exact Verbs | Sentence with Exact Verbs |
|---|---|
| The storm <u>goes</u> through town. | The storm <u>races</u> through town. |

Read the paragraph.  Replace each underlined word with an exact word from the box.  Write the exact words on the lines.

```
pounded      stared        hid
howled       swirled
```

The town was quiet.  Then the wind <u>blew</u> loudly. Leaves <u>went</u> in circles.  Rain <u>fell</u> on the streets.  We <u>put</u> our bags under our coats.  We stayed dry inside the bus stop.  Then the rain stopped.  We <u>looked</u> at a rainbow for a long time.

**1.** blew _____

**2.** went _____

**3.** fell _____

**4.** put _____

**5.** looked _____

**Lesson 9**
PRACTICE BOOK

**How Chipmunk Got His Stripes**
**Phonics:** Base Words and Endings *-ed, -ing*

# Base Words and Endings -ed, -ing

**Read the sentences. Draw a circle around each word that has the ending *-ed* or *-ing*.**

1. Mom is baking a cake for dinner.

2. Dad closed the window when it started to rain.

3. The apple tasted cold and sweet.

4. Jen hoped that her cat was hiding under the bed.

5. The children went hiking last summer.

6. Todd raked the leaves into piles.

**Now write each word you circled under the word that has the same ending.**

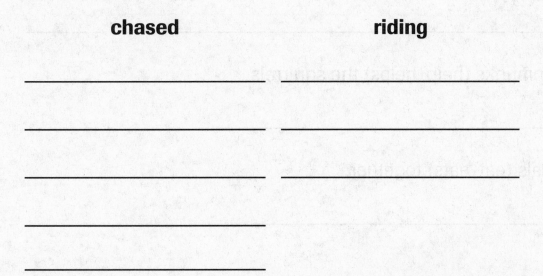

| chased | riding |
|--------|--------|
| _____ | _____ |
| _____ | _____ |
| _____ | _____ |
| _____ |  |

# Adding -*s* to Verbs

A **verb** can name an action that is happening
now.  Add -*s* to this kind of verb when it tells
about a noun that names one.

The <u>chipmunk</u> eat<u>s</u>.
The <u>chipmunks</u> eat.

**Thinking Question**
*Does the subject, or
naming part, of the
sentence name one
or more than one?*

 **Read each sentence. Then write it correctly.**

**1.** The squirrels (see, sees) the chipmunk.

_____

**2.** The chipmunk (share, shares) food.

_____

**3.** A squirrel (run, runs) down the tree.

_____

**4.** More chipmunks (help, helps) the squirrels.

_____

**5.** The animals (eat, eats) together.

_____

# Base Words and Endings
## *-ed, -ing*

**Read each word. Then write the base word and ending on the lines.**

1. hoped _____ + _____

2. skating _____ + _____

3. spilled _____ + _____

4. chasing _____ + _____

5. saving _____ + _____

**Now complete the sentences below with the words from above.**

6. Ling _____ she would get a puppy.

7. Jack is _____ his money to

   get a new mitt.

8. Maria _____ milk on her

   pink dress.

9. The boys like _____ on the

   frozen lake.

10. My cat was _____

    a mouse, but he didn't catch it.

# Understanding Characters

One day Hare said to Tortoise, "You have such short legs, and you walk so slowly. How do you ever get anywhere?"

Tortoise replied, "You are fast, Hare, but if we had a race, I would beat you."

"You could never beat me," laughed Hare.

"Let's have a race," said Tortoise. "You will see."

The race began, and Hare ran much faster than Tortoise. Hare got so far ahead, he thought he had time to take a nap and still win the race.

Tortoise kept moving at a slow, steady pace. He never stopped. When Hare woke up, he saw that Tortoise was ahead of him. Hare ran as fast as he could, but Tortoise won. When Hare crossed the finish line, Tortoise was the one who was napping!

**Read the story. Complete a Column Chart to explain character traits.**

| Words, Actions | What I Know | Character Trait |
|---|---|---|
| Hare | | |
| Tortoise | | |

# -*ed* and -*ing* Endings

Sort the Spelling Words by -*ed* and -*ing* endings.

| -*ed* Endings | -*ing* Endings |
|---|---|
| _____ | _____ |
| _____ | _____ |
| _____ | _____ |
| _____ | _____ |
| _____ | _____ |
| _____ | _____ |

**Add a word you know to each list. Do you need to drop the final *e* before you add -*ed* or -*ing*?**

## Spelling Words

### Basic Words

1. liked
2. using
3. riding
4. chased
5. spilled
6. making
7. closed
8. hoping
9. baked
10. hiding
11. standing
12. asked

### Review Words

13. mixed
14. sleeping

Name _____  Date _____

# Adding -*es* to Verbs

A **verb** can tell about an action that is happening now.  Add -*es* to this kind of verb if it ends with *s, x, ch,* or *sh* and if it tells about a naming part that names one.

The <u>bear</u> mess<u>es</u> the leaf pile.
The <u>bears</u> mess the leaf pile.

**Thinking Question**
*Does the subject name one or more than one?*

 **Read each sentence. Then write it correctly.**

**1.** The mice (fix, fixes) the pile.

_____

**2.** The bear (watch, watches) the mice.

_____

**3.** The bear (push, pushes) the pile down again.

_____

**4.** The mice (wish, wishes) the bear would stop.

_____

**5.** The bear (relax, relaxes) on the pile.

_____

# Focus Trait: Ideas
# Include All Important Steps

Good instructions include all the important steps. Writers leave out steps that are not important.

**Read the steps for each set of instructions. What step do you think is missing? Write the missing step.**

---

**Pouring a Glass of Milk**

Put a glass on a table.

Go to the refrigerator.

Open the refrigerator door.

_____

Pour the milk carefully.

---

**Making Toast**

Get a piece of bread.

Put the bread in the toaster.

Start the toaster.

_____

_____

Spread the butter on the toast.

---

# CV Words

Read each word.  Then write the word and draw a
slash (/) between the two syllables.

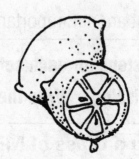

**1.** pilot  _____

**2.** later  _____

**3.** lemon  _____

**4.** hotel  _____

**5.** tiger  _____

Now use the words you wrote above to complete the
sentences below.

**6.** A _____ has orange fur with

black stripes.

**7.** Stan will add _____

to his tea.

**8.** The _____ sits in the front of

the plane.

**9.** We stayed at a big _____ by

the beach last summer.

**10.** Mom likes to stay up _____

than Dad does.

Name _____ Date _____

Lesson 9
PRACTICE BOOK

How Chipmunk Got
His Stripes

Deepen Comprehension:
Understanding Characters

# Understanding Characters

**Read the following story.**

A poor shoemaker said to his wife, "I am tired. I will make these shoes in the morning."

In the morning, the shoemaker saw a pair of new shoes on the table. Someone had made the shoes! Each day, he awoke to find new shoes on the table. The shoemaker got rich.

"We must give a gift to your mystery helper," said his wife. So that night, the shoemaker hid in a corner. He told his wife that he saw two elves make the shoes and run away. She sewed clothes for the elves and left them on the table.

That night, the elves tried on their new clothes. Then they danced out the door and never came back again.

**Complete a Column Chart to tell about the characters.**
**Then answer the following questions.**

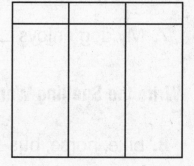

**1.** Think about what the shoemaker's wife says and does. What can you figure out about her?
_____

**2.** Think about the elves' actions. What can you figure out about their traits? _____
_____
_____

# -*ed* and -*ing* Endings

**Use a Spelling Word to complete each sentence.**

1. We _____ the ball down the street.

2. You _____ the play, didn't you?

3. We always keep that door _____ .

4. Matt was _____ he could go to the game.

5. On the first day of school, Ms. Bell _____ us
our names.

6. The game is over, but Ivan is still _____ in
the closet.

7. My dog enjoys _____ near my bed at night.

**Write the Spelling Word that best matches each set of clues.**

8. bike, horse, bus _____

9. leak, drip, tip over _____

10. bread, pie, muffins _____

11. sit, walk, dance _____

12. doze, nap, dream _____

| Spelling Words |
| --- |
| **Basic Words** |
| 1. liked |
| 2. using |
| 3. riding |
| 4. chased |
| 5. spilled |
| 6. making |
| 7. closed |
| 8. hoping |
| 9. baked |
| 10. hiding |
| 11. standing |
| 12. asked |
| **Review Words** |
| 13. mixed |
| 14. sleeping |

# Verbs with -*s* and -*es*

**Draw a line under the verb that completes each sentence correctly.**

**1.** The bear (walk, walks) through the woods.

**2.** The snake (slide, slides) on the ground.

**3.** The rabbit (hop, hops) though the grass.

**4.** The mouse (run, runs) through the field.

**Write the verb correctly to go with the naming part of the sentence.**

**5.** Chipmunk _____ the stew. (mix)

**6.** Squirrel _____ for a spoon. (reach)

**7.** Bear _____ to eat. (rush)

**8.** Bear _____ he had more. (wish)

**Lesson 9**
PRACTICE BOOK

**How Chipmunk Got
His Stripes**
**Vocabulary Strategies:**
Synonyms

Name _____   Date _____

# Synonyms

**Read the sentences.  Choose the word from the box
that means almost the same as the underlined word
and write it on the line.**

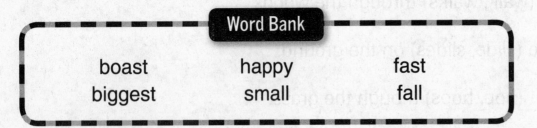

Word Bank

| | | |
|---|---|---|
| boast | happy | fast |
| biggest | small | fall |

1. In <u>autumn</u>, the leaves change colors.

    _____

2. The elephant is the <u>largest</u> animal at the zoo.

    _____

3. The mouse is very <u>little</u>.

    _____

4. Anita was <u>glad</u> to see her best friend.

    _____

5. The runner was <u>quick</u>, so he won the race.

    _____

6. Hans likes to <u>brag</u> when he wins a game.

    _____

# Proofread for Spelling

**Proofread the story. Cross out the six misspelled words. Spell it correctly above the word you crossed out.**

Tomorrow school will be klosed, so we are going

bike ridin along the lake to the next town. All of us

have been makeing plans for a long time. My brother

bakked some cookies to take along. I am useing my

dad's backpack to carry sandwiches and juice, but I

haven't aksed him yet!

**Use the code to spell the Spelling Words.**

| 1 = e | 2 = s | 3 = i | 4 = n | 5 = d | 6 = a | 7 = k |
|-------|-------|-------|-------|-------|-------|-------|
| 8 = p | 9 = m | 10 = o | 11 = 5 | 12 = b | 13 = t | 14 = u |
| 15 = c | 16 = j | 17 = h | 18 = f | 19 = r | 20 = l | 21 = g |
| 22 = x | 23 = z | 24 = y | 25 = q | 26 = w | | |

**1.** 6-2-7-1-5 _____    **3.** 15-17-6-2-1-5 _____

**2.** 17-3-5-3-4-21 _____    **4.** 20-3-7-1-5 _____

## Spelling Words

**Basic Words**
1. liked
2. using
3. riding
4. chased
5. spilled
6. making
7. closed
8. hoping
9. baked
10. hiding
11. standing
12. asked

**Lesson 9**
PRACTICE BOOK

**How Chipmunk Got
His Stripes**
**Grammar:** Spiral Review

# Kinds of Nouns

✏️ **Draw a line under the noun in each sentence.**
**Write whether it names a person, place, thing, or animal.**

**1.** The dog growls. _____

**2.** The tree stands tall. _____

**3.** Sally looks out. _____

**4.** The yard is busy. _____

✏️ **Read the paragraph. Write a noun from the box in place of each underlined noun.**

| forest | mouse | owl | rock |
|--------|-------|-----|------|

    The <u>place</u> is dark. An owl looks for food to eat.
It sees a mouse near a big <u>thing</u>. The owl swoops down
and lands on the rock. It wants to catch the <u>animal</u>.
The mouse quickly scurries into a small space under the
rock. It is safe! The <u>animal</u> flies back up to its nest.

**5.** place _____    **7.** animal _____

**6.** thing _____    **8.** animal _____

# Sentence Fluency

| Short Sentences | New Sentence with Joined Predicates |
|---|---|
| The bear sees honey.<br>The bear eats it all. | The bear sees honey and eats it all. |

Join each pair of sentences.  Use *and* between the predicates.  Then write the new sentence.

**1.** The squirrels climb the tree.

The squirrels eat some nuts.

_____

**2.** The deer eats leaves.

The deer drinks from the pond.

_____

**3.** Chipmunks rest on rocks.

Chipmunks sleep on leaves.

_____

**4.** The lion runs fast.

The lion looks for food.

_____

# Contractions

**Put the words together to write contractions. Then read
each contraction.**

1. you + are = _____

2. is + not = _____

3. we + will = _____

4. it + is = _____

5. do + not = _____

6. I + am = _____

**Use the contractions you wrote above
to complete the sentences below.**

7. The sun _____ going to
   shine today.

8. I think _____ going to rain all day.

9. _____ have to stay inside.

10. I hope _____ planning to
    come over to my house.

11. I _____ know what we can play.

12. _____ sure we can think of
    something to do.

# Past Time Verbs with -*ed*

Some **verbs** name actions that are happening now.  Other **verbs** name actions that happened before now, or in the past. Add -*ed* to most verbs to show that the action happened in the past.

Yesterday the jellyfish (float, <u>floated</u>) in the water.

**Thinking Question**
*When does or did the action happen?*

**Read each sentence.  Choose the verb that tells about the past.  Then rewrite the sentence.**

**1.** Fish (pass, passed) by the jellyfish.

_____

**2.** Sea turtles (splashed, splash) near the fish.

_____

**3.** Whales (leap, leaped) over the sea turtles.

_____

**4.** The sharks (watched, watch) the animals move.

_____

# Contractions

Use the two words below the line to make a contraction. Write the contraction on the line. Then read each completed sentence.

1. I _____ know how to skate.
   do not

2. _____ more fun to ride my bike.
   It is

3. I _____ find my knee pads.
   did not

4. _____ try to find my helmet.
   I will

5. Then _____ have fun on our bikes.
   we will

Draw a circle around the contraction in each sentence.
Then write the two words for each contraction.

6. I'm going to the store. _____

7. If you're ready, you can go, too. _____

8. The store isn't too far away. _____

9. We'll need to buy milk and meat. _____

10. I don't think I can carry it on my bike! _____

Name _____ Date _____

Lesson 10
PRACTICE BOOK

Jellies
Introduce Comprehension:
Fact and Opinion

# Fact and Opinion

Coral reefs are found in some oceans. These reefs are made by tiny animals. When these tiny animals die, they leave behind piles of empty shells. More tiny animals grow on top of these shells. This happens over and over again. The coral reef gets bigger and bigger.

You can dive near a coral reef! Everything you see will be beautiful. You might even see green sea turtles. They are a little bit scary, though. They are about three feet long and weigh about 300 pounds.

You may also see colorful angelfish. They aren't afraid as they swim around. They can hide inside cracks in the coral if they need to be safe.

**Read the article above. Then complete a T-Map that lists three facts and three opinions from the article.**

| Fact | Opinion |
|---|---|
| _____ | _____ |
| _____ | _____ |
| _____ | _____ |
| _____ | _____ |
| _____ | _____ |
| _____ | _____ |

# Contractions

Sort the Spelling Words by the word used to make each contraction. The first one is done for you.

| with *not* | with *is* | with *have* |
|---|---|---|
| don't | _____ | _____ |
| _____ | _____ | _____ |
| _____ | | |
| _____ | | |

| with *am* | with *will* | with *are* |
|---|---|---|
| _____ | _____ | _____ |
| _____ | _____ | _____ |
| _____ | _____ | _____ |

## Spelling Words

### Basic Words
1. I'm
2. don't
3. isn't
4. can't
5. we'll
6. it's
7. I've
8. didn't
9. you're
10. that's
11. wasn't
12. you've

### Review Words
13. us
14. them

**Then add three contractions that you know to any of the lists.**

**Lesson 10**
PRACTICE BOOK

**Jellies**
**Grammar:** Verbs in the Present,
Past, and Future

# Verbs in Future Time

Some **verbs** name actions that are going to
happen.  Add *will* before a verb to show that
the action is going to happen in the future.

| | |
|---|---|
| The sea turtles <u>want</u> food. | **Present** |
| The sea turtles <u>will want</u> food. | **Future** |

**Thinking Question**
*When does or did
the action happen?*

  Decide how to make each underlined verb show that
the action happens in the future. Then rewrite the sentence.

**1.** The sea turtles <u>rush</u> past the whale.

_____

**2.** The waves <u>wash</u> over the beach.

_____

**3.** The jellyfish <u>drift</u> out to sea.

_____

**4.** Sea birds <u>swoop</u> down.

_____

**141**

Name _____ Date _____

# Focus Trait: Word Choice
# Using Exact Words

**Using synonyms is one way to rewrite sentences in your own words.**

| When it stings, a jellyfish <u>does not know</u> if it is hurting a <u>friend</u> or an <u>enemy</u>. | When it stings, a jellyfish <u>is not aware</u> if it is hurting a <u>buddy</u> or a <u>rival</u>. |
|---|---|

**Read each sentence. Replace each underlined word with a synonym.**

| | |
|---|---|
| **1.** The ocean is a <u>huge</u> place. | |
| **2.** There are many <u>strange creatures</u> in the ocean. | |
| **3.** Getting stung by a jellyfish can be <u>painful</u>. | |
| **4.** Jellyfish are <u>beautiful</u>. | |
| **5.** Special plants <u>survive</u> underwater in the ocean. | |

# Cumulative Review

Read each sentence.  Choose the word from the box
that completes each sentence and write the word on
the line.  Then read each completed sentence.

**Word Bank**

| | | | |
|---|---|---|---|
| fishing | shining | flashed | then |
| wished | chasing | think | path |

**1.** The sun was _____.

**2.** Dale and Jack wanted to go _____.

**3.** The boys walked along a _____.

**4.** Jack _____ they would get to
the lake soon.

**5.** Just _____, a rabbit ran by.

**6.** The bunny _____ its white tail.

**7.** Dale didn't _____ rabbits
could run that fast.

**8.** Was someone _____ it?

**Now write on the line a word you know that begins with each
letter pair.**

**9.** ch _____   **10.** sh _____

# Facts and Opinions

**Read the selection below.**

I went to the library to learn more about dolphins. I read books and looked on the Internet, too. I learned a lot.

Some people think that dolphins are always happy. That's because it looks like they're smiling all the time. But dolphins aren't always happy. The shape of their mouths just looks like a smile.

Dolphins are playful. Scientists say that dolphins play all day long. Some dolphins love to play with balls and hoops. They love their trainers, too. I think it would be fun to play with dolphins!

**Complete a T-Map like the one here to list facts and opinions. Then answer the questions below.**

**1.** What sentence in this selection told a fact?

_____

_____

**2.** What sentence in this selection told an opinion?

_____

_____

# Contractions

**Write the Spelling Word that has the same meaning.**

1. you are _____

2. cannot _____

3. I am _____

4. is not _____

5. we will _____

6. you have _____

7. it is _____

8. I have _____

**Read each sentence. Think about the underlined word or words. Then write the Spelling Word that makes the sentence say the opposite.**

9. I <u>did</u> make my bed.                    _____

10. <u>That is</u> <u>not</u> my book.             _____

11. Sara <u>was</u> late to school.             _____

12. <u>You are</u> <u>not</u> my friends.          _____

13. <u>I am</u> <u>not</u> asking Miguel.          _____

14. I <u>do</u> have time to spend with you.  _____

**Spelling Words**

**Basic Words**

1. I'm
2. don't
3. isn't
4. can't
5. we'll
6. it's
7. I've
8. didn't
9. you're
10. that's
11. wasn't
12. you've

**Review Words**

13. us
14. them

# Present, Past, and Future Time

Rewrite each sentence. Change the verb so it tells that the action happened at the time shown.

1. The sea animals <u>want</u> food. (action in past)

_____

2. The crabs <u>searched</u> for small fish. (action in present)

_____

3. The jellyfish <u>look</u> under a big rock. (action in past)

_____

4. Waves <u>wash</u> away the sand castle. (action in future)

_____

5. Max and Beth <u>play</u> in the water. (action in future)

_____

6. They <u>peek</u> inside a shell. (action in future)

_____

# Suffixes -*er*, -*est*

**Circle the comparing word that completes each sentence.**

**1.** A mouse is **smaller    smallest**  than a cat.

**2.** I am going to exercise so I get
**stronger    strongest**.

**3.** That is the **bigger    biggest**  spider I have
ever seen!

**4.** Being sick made me feel **weaker    weakest**
than I did before.

**5.** Juan wants to be the **smarter    smartest**
student in the class.

**6.** That side of the pool is **shallower    shallowest**
than this side.

**7.** Chocolate is the **sweeter    sweetest**  kind of
ice cream.

# Proofread for Spelling

**Rewrite each sentence. Use two contractions in each sentence.**

**1.** I am sure he did not see me.

_____

**2.** That is where you are going.

_____

**3.** It is our class picnic, so we will go early.

_____

**Proofread the note. Cross out the six misspelled contractions. Spell each word correctly in the margin.**

| Spelling Words |
| --- |
| **Basic Words** |
| 1. I'm |
| 2. don't |
| 3. isn't |
| 4. can't |
| 5. we'll |
| 6. it's |
| 7. I've |
| 8. didn't |
| 9. you're |
| 10. that's |
| 11. wasn't |
| 12. you've |

Dear Pam,

I kan't go tomorrow because I'ave got too much

homework. I know yo'uve been counting on me.

Maybe I can come over later in the evening. Then wi'll

have time to talk. I hope its' OK. I'am

going to start my math problems right now.

Sincerely,

Carmen

Name _____ Date _____

# Singular and Plural Nouns

Draw a line under the noun in each sentence.
If the noun names one, write *S* for *singular*. If the noun
names more than one, write *P* for *plural*.

1. The sharks swim fast. _____

2. Four girls watch. _____

3. One boy points. _____

4. A girl looks again. _____

5. The animals are gone now. _____

Read each sentence. Then rewrite each underlined
noun in the correct plural form.

6. Look at the crab. _____

7. Do not touch the claw. _____

8. Tell the adult to come quickly. _____

9. The boy can use help. _____

10. The crabs crawled in the bag. _____

# Sentence Fluency

| Verbs Telling About Different Times | Verbs Telling the Same Time |
|---|---|
| Last week Jill and Jake <u>walked</u> on the beach. They <u>play</u> in the water. | Last week Jill and Jake <u>walked</u> on the beach. They <u>played</u> in the water. |

**Read this story. It tells about something that happened in the past. Five verbs do not tell about the past. Fix these five verbs. Then write the story correctly on the lines below.**

Jill and Jake skipped along the shore. Jake saw two large shells. Jake point to them. Jill rush over to see them. Jill and Jake look closely. Jill pick up one shell. Jill and Jake wash the shells and took them home.

_____

_____

_____

_____

_____

Name _____ Date _____

Lesson 11
PRACTICE BOOK

Click, Clack, Moo:
Cows That Type
**Phonics:** Base Words and
Endings *-s, -es*

# Base Words and Endings
## *-s, -es*

**Put the letters together to write a base word.**
**Then add the ending *-s* or *-es*.**

**1.** m + a + t + c + h = _____

**2.** b + u + z + z = _____

**3.** g + l + a + s + s = _____

**4.** b + u + s + h = _____

**5.** h + a + m + m + e + r = _____

**Now use the words you wrote above to complete the**
**sentences below.**

**6.** Dad _____ the nails into

the wall.

**7.** I drank two _____ of milk

for dinner.

**8.** Today my jacket _____ my hat.

**9.** My dog likes to hide in the _____.

**10.** The bee _____ near the hive.

**Lesson 11**
PRACTICE BOOK

**Click, Clack, Moo:
Cows That Type**
**Grammar:** Kinds of Sentences

# Commands

- A **command** is a sentence that tells a person or animal to do something.
- A command begins with a capital letter and ends with a period.
- A command usually begins with an action word.

Example: Come with me.

**Thinking Question**
*Does the sentence begin with an action word?*

 **Write each command correctly.**

**1.** feed the animals

_____

**2.** hold the pail

_____

**3.** pet the cows

_____

**4.** talk to the chickens

_____

**5.** sweep the stable

_____

# Base Words and Endings -*s*, -*es*

Write the words from the box under the word that has the same ending. Then write two more words of your own in each column.

.................... **Word Bank** ....................

| eggs | trucks | brushes | fixes |
| wishes | tigers | pinches | rafts |

<u>lunch</u>es                              <u>chick</u>s

_____        _____

_____        _____

_____        _____

_____        _____

_____        _____

**Lesson 11**
PRACTICE BOOK

**Click, Clack, Moo:
Cows That Type**

Introduce Comprehension:
Conclusions

# Conclusions

Kathy the Crow was tired of looking for her own food. She saw a pile of grain by the henhouse. She flew low and cried, "Caw! Caw!" The hens and little chicks ran inside.

Kathy landed by a pile of grain and began to eat.

Suddenly, she saw a flash of red! A big red wing came flapping her way and scared her away from the grain. Kathy flew off into the sky!

"You can come out," Rooster called to the hens. "I don't think Kathy will be stopping for lunch again!"

**Read the selection above. Add another story clue to the Inference Map below that will help you draw a conclusion about Rooster and what he did.**

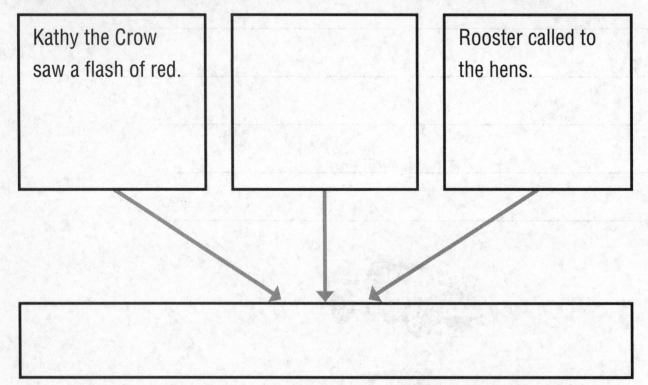

| Kathy the Crow saw a flash of red. | | Rooster called to the hens. |

Name _____ Date _____

# Base Words with Endings -*s*, -*es*

**Click, Clack, Moo: Cows That Type**
**Spelling:** Base Words with Endings -*s*, -*es*

Sort the Spelling Words by -*s* and -*es* endings. Then draw a line under each word ending that changed the word from meaning one to meaning more than one.

**Words with -*s* Endings**          **Words with -*es* Endings**

1. _____      11. _____

2. _____      12. _____

3. _____      13. _____

4. _____      14. _____

5. _____

6. _____

7. _____

8. _____

9. _____

10. _____

## Spelling Words

**Basic Words**

1. hens
2. eggs
3. ducks
4. bikes
5. boxes
6. wishes
7. dresses
8. names
9. bells
10. stamps
11. dishes
12. grapes

**Review Words**

13. jets
14. frogs

# Three Kinds of Sentences

- A **question** asks something.

- A **statement** tells something.

- A **command** tells someone
  to do something.

| | |
|---|---|
| What can the cow do? | **Question** |
| The cow can type. | **Statement** |
| Watch that cow type. | **Command** |

**Thinking Question**
*Does the sentence
tell, ask, or command
something?*

✏ **Read each sentence. Then label it as a question,
statement, or command.**

**1.** What does the horse do?

_____

**2.** The horse tells jokes.

_____

**3.** Listen to this joke.

_____

**4.** Have you heard that joke before?

_____

# Focus Trait: Ideas
# Stating a Clear Goal

| Not a Clear Goal | Clear Goal |
|---|---|
| I would like you to <u>do something.</u> | I would like you to **take me to the park next weekend.** |

**A. Read each goal that is not clear. Fill in the blanks to state each goal more clearly.**

| Not a Clear Goal | Clear Goal |
|---|---|
| **1.** I would like you to buy <u>something</u> for our computer lab. | I would like you to _____ for our computer lab. |
| **2.** I want you to send me <u>stuff</u> for a project. | I want you to send me _____ for a project. |

**B. Read each goal that is not clear. Add a word or words to make the goal more clear. Write your new sentences.**

| Not a Clear Goal | Clear Goal |
|---|---|
| **3.** We would like you to <u>do us a favor.</u> | |
| **4.** I am writing to ask you <u>to do something</u> for the music room. | |

Name _____ Date _____

**Lesson 11**
PRACTICE BOOK

**Click, Clack, Moo:
Cows That Type**
**Phonics:** Cumulative Review

# Cumulative Review

**Write the word that goes in each sentence.**

.......... **Word Bank** ..........

cider  fever  later  virus

1. Jack has a _____ that makes him sick.

2. Mom says his _____ is very high.

3. "You can sit with Jack _____ today," said Mom.

4. "I'll warm up some _____ for both of you," said Mom.

**Write the words that make up each underlined contraction.**

5. "I won't have lunch with Sam today," said Jack.

   _____.

6. "I'll tell Sam you miss him, Jack," I said.

   _____.

7. "You're a good sister," said Jack.

   _____.

Name _____ Date _____

**Lesson 11**
PRACTICE BOOK

**Click, Clack, Moo:
Cows That Type**

**Deepen Comprehension:**
Conclusions

# Conclusions

**Read the selection below.**

The trees were red, so Squirrel began picking up nuts.

"Squirrel," said Red Hen, "you're very smart. When winter comes, you'll have lots to eat."

"Thank you," said Squirrel. Squirrel boasted to Chipmunk, "I'm smart! I'm smart!" Then Squirrel began racing around, burying his nuts as fast as he could.

The rains came. Then the snow fell. Squirrel dug under the trees for his nuts. But where were they? Squirrel couldn't remember.

"Next year, make a map in your head," said Chipmunk.

"I think they're between the big rocks," said Red Hen.

"Oh, thank you, Red Hen," said Squirrel. "How did you remember?"

"Shh!" said Red Hen. "That's where I hide my eggs! Don't tell Farmer Brown!"

**Now complete an Inference Map to draw a conclusion about why Squirrel forgets where he puts the nuts.**

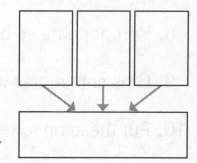

**1.** Why does Squirrel get so excited?

_____

**2.** What happens when Squirrel gets so excited?

_____

_____

Lesson 11
PRACTICE BOOK

Click, Clack, Moo:
Cows That Type
Spelling: Base Words with
Endings -s, -es

# Base Words with Endings -s, -es

Write the Spelling Word or Spelling Words that match each clue.

1. These are animals. _____

_____ _____

2. You can eat these. _____

_____

3. Put things inside these. _____

4. Put food on these. _____

5. Ride on these. _____

6. These ring. _____

7. These are airplanes. _____

8. You hope these come true. _____

9. Girls sometimes wear these. _____

10. Put these on letters. _____

11. We give pets these. _____

## Spelling Words

**Basic Words**
1. hens
2. eggs
3. ducks
4. bikes
5. boxes
6. wishes
7. dresses
8. names
9. bells
10. stamps
11. dishes
12. grapes

**Review Words**
13. jets
14. frogs

# Three Kinds of Sentences

 **Write each command correctly.**

**1.** play with me

_____

**2.** hide in the barn

_____

**3.** do not peek

_____

**Label each sentence as a question, a statement, or a
command. Then write the sentence correctly.**

**4.** look out _____

_____

**5.** i almost dropped the eggs _____

_____

**6.** can you help me _____

_____

# Prefixes *pre-* and *mis-*

Read each definition below. Add *mis-* or *pre-* to a
word in the box to make a new word that matches each
definition.

### Word Bank

| | | |
|---|---|---|
| heard | judge | read |
| order | heat | |

**1.** to order before _____

**2.** to judge badly _____

**3.** to heat before _____

**4.** did not read right _____

**5.** did not hear right _____

## Write a sentence for each word.

**6. misdial** _____

_____

**7. precut** _____

_____

**Lesson 11**
PRACTICE BOOK

# Proofread for Spelling

**Click, Clack, Moo:
Cows That Type**
**Spelling:** Base Words with
Endings -*s*, -*es*

**Proofread the newspaper story. Circle the nine
misspelled words. Then write the correct spellings.**

### Wishs Come True

    Mr. and Mrs. Smith kept birds in a pen. Saturday,
they rode their biks. Then they checked the pen. They
found only empty boxees. "I wanted to ring alarm belz,"
said Mr. Smith. "I wish that we would find our birds."

    When they went inside the house, they found the
duks sleeping on Mrs. Smith's dreses, and the henz had
laid egs on her new dishis!

| Spelling Words |
| --- |
| **Basic Words** |
| 1. hens |
| 2. eggs |
| 3. ducks |
| 4. bikes |
| 5. boxes |
| 6. wishes |
| 7. dresses |
| 8. names |
| 9. bells |
| 10. stamps |
| 11. dishes |
| 12. grapes |

1. _____  6. _____

2. _____  7. _____

3. _____  8. _____

4. _____  9. _____

5. _____

**Unscramble the letters to spell a Basic Word.**

10. pgares _____  12. pmasts _____

11. maens _____

# More Plural Nouns

 **Circle the noun that correctly shows more than one.**

**1.** We eat (sandwichs, sandwiches) in the barn.

**2.** Our (dresss, dresses) get dirty.

**3.** The (mouses, mice) play in the hay.

**4.** The (horse, horses) stomp their feet.

**5.** The (cow, cows) stand still.

**Read each sentence. Then rewrite each sentence to use the correct plural form of the underlined noun.**

**6.** Two <u>fox</u> visit the farm.

_____

**7.** Many <u>man</u> help plant seeds.

_____

**8.** How many <u>child</u> are in your school?

_____

# Sentence Fluency

| Run-on Sentence | Separate Sentences |
|---|---|
| The horse runs fast can the cow run too? | The horse runs fast. Can the cow run too? |

| Run-on Sentence | Separate Sentences |
|---|---|
| Help me get eggs we will go to the barn. | Help me get eggs. We will go to the barn. |

Read the run-on sentences. Turn each one into two separate sentences. Write the two new sentences.

**1.** We collect milk there are a lot of cows.

_____

**2.** We need eggs where are the chickens.

_____

**3.** Find some seeds the ducks are hungry.

_____

**4.** Look at the pigs they are happy.

_____

**5.** The farm is busy we also have fun.

_____

# Words with *ai, ay*

**Write a word from the box to complete each sentence.**

.................. Word Bank ..................

pail          maybe          say
tail          play           wait

1. I like to _____ games with my

   dog Spot.

2. "Come here, Spot," I _____.

3. Spot jumps up and wags his _____.

4. _____ Spot will run after a ball.

5. I tossed the ball, and it landed in a _____.

6. Spot fetches the ball while I _____

   for him.

**Now write each word under the word that has the same**
**pattern for long *a*.**

| **ma̲i̲l** | **da̲y̲** |
|---|---|
| _____ | _____ |
| _____ | _____ |
| _____ | _____ |

# Exclamations

- All sentences begin with a capital letter.

- An **exclamation** is one kind of sentence. It ends with an **exclamation point (!).**

- An exclamation shows a strong feeling such as excitement, surprise, or fear.

Example: Gina loves music!

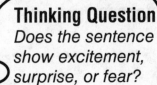

**Thinking Question**
*Does the sentence show excitement, surprise, or fear?*

 **Draw a line under each correct exclamation.**

**1.** Gina is a wonderful singer!

Gina is a singer.

**2.** She also plays the piano.

She also plays the piano so well!

**3.** She is going to star in the show!

She is going to be in the show.

**4.** Let's go see her sing!

Let's go see her.

**5.** I will save you a great seat!

I will save you a seat.

Name _____  Date _____

# Words with *ai, ay*

**Read the letter. Draw a circle around the words with *ai* and *ay*. Then write two sentences to finish the letter. Choose two words from the box to use in your sentences.**

> **Word Bank**
>
> | rain | hail | day | may |
> |------|------|-----|-----|
> | gray | mail | pay | trail |

Dear Jay,

    Today my class went on a trip. I could not wait!
We saw people make crafts. A man made pots out of
clay. One woman wove a braid for a rug. The people
sell their crafts and then they get paid. _____

_____

_____

_____

       Your friend,

       _____

# Story Structure

Jodi loved to teach tricks to her pets. When she was three, she showed her dog how to roll over. When she was five, she showed her hamster how to climb the curtains. Now Jodi was eight and wanted to win the Pet Tricks Contest. She showed her parrot Billy the best trick yet.

Jodi's friend Mel came over to meet Billy.

Billy squawked, "Billy wants a cracker!"

"That's not very special," said Mel. "I don't think you'll win."

"Just wait," said Jodi. She began singing "Yankee Doodle Dandy." So did Billy. Jodi stopped singing, but Billy kept going. He sang the whole song by himself!

"Wow!" said Mel. "Now that's a winning pet trick!"

**Read the story above. Complete a Story Map to identify parts of the story.**

| **Characters:** Jodi, Mel, Billy | **Setting:** Jodi's home |
|---|---|
| **Problem:** Jodi wants to enter Billy in the Pet Trick Contest, but Mel doesn't think the parrot will win. ||
| **Events:** 1. _____ <br> 2. _____ <br> 3. _____ <br> 4. _____ ||
| **Solution:** Mel feels this trick will win the contest. ||

# Words with *ai, ay*

Sort the Spelling Words by the long *a* sound spelled *ai* and the long *a* sound spelled *ay*.

**Basic Words**
1. pay
2. wait
3. paint
4. train
5. pail
6. clay
7. tray
8. plain
9. stain
10. hay
11. gray
12. away

**Review Words**
13. stay
14. day

| *ai* Words | *ay* Words |
|---|---|
| 1. _____ | 7. _____ |
| 2. _____ | 8. _____ |
| 3. _____ | 9. _____ |
| 4. _____ | 10. _____ |
| 5. _____ | 11. _____ |
| 6. _____ | 12. _____ |
| | 13. _____ |
| | 14. _____ |

Underline the letters in each word that make the long *a* sound.

# Four Kinds of Sentences

| | |
|---|---|
| A **question** asks something. | Will you sing with me? |
| An **exclamation** shows strong feeling. | It will be fun! |
| A **command** tells someone to do something. | Stand up. |
| A **statement** tells something. | We can start now. |

**Thinking Question**
*Does the sentence ask, tell, command, or show strong feeling?*

 **Read each sentence. Tell what kind of sentence it is.**

**1.** We will sing songs. _____

**2.** Can you join us? _____

**3.** Count to three. _____

**4.** That was so great! _____

**5.** When can we do it again? _____

**6.** I loved singing! _____

# Focus Trait: Voice
# Showing Feelings

| Weak Voice | Strong Voice |
|---|---|
| I like movie music. | Movie music is so great to listen to! |

**A. Read each sentence that has a weak voice. Add or change some words to make the voice stronger.**

| Weak Voice | Strong Voice |
|---|---|
| **1.** The guitar is a musical instrument. | The guitar is a _____ musical instrument. |
| **2.** I like all music. | Any kind of music _____ _____ |

**B. Read each sentence that has a weak voice. Add words to make the voice stronger. Write your new sentences.**

| Weak Voice | Strong Voice |
|---|---|
| **3.** Our band played a concert. | _____ _____ |
| **4.** The trumpet is a good instrument. | _____ _____ |

# Cumulative Review

**Write the word that goes in each sentence.**

Word Bank

| snails | boxes | glasses | bikes |

1. "I can't lift these big _____ of books," said Meg.

2. "We'll ride our _____ to school," Rick said.

3. "I've filled three _____ with milk," said Max.

4. "You're moving at the speed of _____ this morning," Mom said.

**Now write each word from the Word Bank under the word that has the same ending.**

**paints**                    **patches**

_____        _____

_____        _____

Name _____     Date _____

Lesson 12
PRACTICE BOOK

Violet's Music
Deepen Comprehension:
Story Structure

# Story Structure

**Read the selection below.**

Joe was waiting for his turn.  The class sang, "Hickory dickory dock.  The mouse ran up the clock."  Amy made her mouse puppet run around the clock.  Everyone clapped.

Then the class sang, "The clock struck one.  The mouse ran down."  It was Joe's turn!

Joe banged on the gong.  But he banged it too hard.  Its noise was so loud that Joe fell over.  As he fell, Joe banged into Amy, and she fell over.  Then Amy hit the clock and it fell over!

"Hickory dickory dock!" sang the class.

Everyone clapped!  They thought it was the funniest show they'd ever seen. Joe laughed so hard that he forgot all about his mistake.

**Now complete a Story Map and answer the following questions.**

1. Who are the characters in this story?
   Where does this story take place?

_____

_____

2. How is Joe's problem solved at the end of the story?

_____

# Words with *ai, ay*

**Basic Words**
1. pay
2. wait
3. paint
4. train
5. pail
6. clay
7. tray
8. plain
9. stain
10. hay
11. gray
12. away

**Review Words**
13. stay
14. day

**Read each word aloud. Then write the Spelling Word or Spelling Words that rhyme with the word.**

1. main _____    _____

_____    _____

2. faint _____

3. play _____    _____

_____    _____

_____    _____

# Kinds of Sentences

| | |
|---|---|
| A **question** ends with a question mark. | Will you sing with me? |
| An **exclamation** ends with an exclamation point. | It will be fun! |
| A **command** ends with a period. | Stand up. |
| A **statement** ends with a period. | We can start now. |

 **Read each sentence. Tell what kind of sentence it is.**
**Then rewrite each sentence with the correct end mark.**

**1.** marco plays guitar _____

_____

**2.** where is he _____

_____

**3.** ask him to join our band _____

_____

**4.** that is a great idea _____

_____

# Idioms

**Read the sentence.  Choose the idiom from the box that could replace the underlined words.  Write the idiom.**

> **Word Bank**
>
> step on it          cry my eyes out          get the picture
> shake a leg          run like the wind          hang in there

**1.** We were late for school, so Dad told us to <u>hurry up</u>.

_____

**2.** I kept striking out, but my coach told me to <u>keep trying</u>.

_____

**3.** Mike explained to Tina how to play the game.

"Do you <u>understand</u>?" he asked.

_____

**4.** My best friend is moving away.  I am so sad I feel like

I could <u>cry forever</u>.

_____

**5.** We need to leave soon, so <u>get moving</u>!

_____

**6.** I'm going to <u>run really fast</u> so I can win the race.

_____

# Proofread for Spelling

Proofread the journal entry. Circle the ten misspelled words. Then write the correct spellings on the lines below.

Today was fun. I helped paynt my room. I couldn't wate to start. My walls were plane grae. Dad had a payl of blue paint. He showed me how to use a paint brush and trai. We had to be neat so paint would not stane my carpet. We made the gray go awai. Then we drew a trane passing a farm with hae stacks on the wall.

| | | | |
|---|---|---|---|
| 1. _____ | | 6. _____ | |
| 2. _____ | | 7. _____ | |
| 3. _____ | | 8. _____ | |
| 4. _____ | | 9. _____ | |
| 5. _____ | | 10. _____ | |

**Spelling Words**

**Basic Words**
1. pay
2. wait
3. paint
4. train
5. pail
6. clay
7. tray
8. plain
9. stain
10. hay
11. gray
12. away

**Review Words**
13. stay
14. day

Read the following sentences. Circle each misspelled word. Then write it correctly.

**11.** We bought modeling claie at the store. _____

**12.** I had a gift card to pa for it. _____

# Writing Proper Nouns

Write the proper noun in each sentence correctly on the line.

**1.** My friend jessica plays the flute. _____

**2.** She will play in a concert with rick. _____

**3.** The concert is in chicago. _____

**4.** She will bring her dog willy. _____

Read each sentence.  Choose the correct proper noun to replace the underlined words.  Write the new sentence on the line.

**5.** The woman loves the piano. (Carmen, Canada)

_____

**6.** She plays it for her fish. (New Mexico, Bubbles)

_____

**7.** People on the street hear the song. (Cherry Lane, Mary)

_____

**8.** The man sings to the tune. (David, Carrie)

_____

# Sentence Fluency

| Short, Choppy Sentences | Longer, Smoother Sentence |
|---|---|
| Margo plays the piano.  Luis sings in Spanish. | Margo plays the piano, and Luis sings in Spanish. |

| Short, Choppy Sentences | Longer, Smoother Sentence |
|---|---|
| Luis takes singing lessons.  His mom drives him there. | Luis takes singing lessons, and his mom drives him there. |

**Rewrite each pair of sentences.  Use *and* to join them into one longer sentence.  Put a comma before *and*.**

1. Tim plays the violin.  The crowd claps.

_____

2. Dana reads music.  Doug learns from her.

_____

3. Mom plays guitar.  She teaches Manny to play.

_____

4. Dad plays the drums.  We listen to the beat.

_____

5. We like music.  We love to play together.

_____

Name _____  Date _____

# Words with *ee, ea*

**Write a word for each clue.**

**1.** It rhymes with *see.*

It begins like *bat.* _____

**2.** It rhymes with *beaches.*

It begins like *pig.* _____

**3.** It rhymes with *sweet.*

It begins like *mail.* _____

**4.** It rhymes with *sheep.*

It begins like *kitten.* _____

**5.** It rhymes with *beast.*

It begins like *fox.* _____

**6.** It rhymes with *clean.*

It begins like *bay.* _____

**Use two of the words you wrote above in sentences of your own.**

**7.** _____

**8.** _____

# Using Quotation Marks

When you write, show what someone says by putting **quotation marks (" ")** at the beginning and end of the speaker's exact words.

Luis said, "I play the drums."
Kim said, "I play the guitar."

**Thinking Question**
*What are the speaker's exact words?*

✏ **Write each sentence. Put quotation marks around the speaker's exact words.**

**1.** Jamal asked, Will you play for me?

_____

**2.** Luis said, We will play for you.

_____

**3.** Kim asked, Do you play, too?

_____

**4.** Jamal answered, I play the piano.

_____

**5.** The kids said, Come play with us!

_____

Name _____  Date _____

# Words with *ee, ea*

**Read the sentences. Draw a circle around each word
that has the long *e* sound spelled *ee* or *ea*.**

**1.** A creek is a small river or stream.

**2.** We ate roast beef and green beans.

**3.** The wheels on the car  squeak.

**4.** If you heat a pot of water, you can make steam.

**5.** We clean our home every week.

**Now write each word you circled under the word that has the
same spelling for the long *e* sound.**

| **speed** | **beach** |
|-----------|-----------|
| _____ | _____ |
| _____ | _____ |
| _____ | _____ |
| _____ | _____ |
|           | _____ |

**Lesson 13**
PRACTICE BOOK

**Schools Around
the World**
**Introduce Comprehension:**
Author's Purpose

# Author's Purpose

Would you like to get your hands dirty at school?  Some schools have their own gardens.  The children decide what to grow.  They learn how to plant seeds.

The children must water the plants and pull weeds in their gardens.  They learn about good bugs and bad bugs, too.

Once the plants are grown, children get to pick what they grew.  If they grew food, they can cook it and eat it.

School gardens are a good way to get fresh air and exercise.  Children who plant gardens also enjoy eating the healthful foods that they grow.  Gardening at school can be healthy and fun, too!

**Read the selection above.  Ask yourself questions about the author's purpose for writing this selection.  Then write details in the boxes that helped you decide the author's purpose.**

| The author tells what children do in school gardens. | | The author tells how gardening is healthy and fun. |
|---|---|---|

**Author's Purpose:**

# Words with *ee, ea*

*ee*             *ea*

**Sort the Spelling Words by *ee* and *ea* spellings.**

| ***ee* Words** | ***ea* Words** |
| --- | --- |
| 1. _____ | 6. _____ |
| 2. _____ | 7. _____ |
| 3. _____ | 8. _____ |
| 4. _____ | 9. _____ |
| 5. _____ | 10. _____ |
| | 11. _____ |
| | 12. _____ |
| | 13. _____ |
| | 14. _____ |

**Underline the letters in each word that make the long *e* sound.**

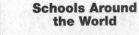

**Spelling Words**

**Basic
Words**
1. free
2. teach
3. teeth
4. please
5. beach
6. wheel
7. team
8. speak
9. sneeze
10. sheep
11. meaning
12. weave

**Review
Words**
13. eat
14. read

Spelling      **185**      Grade 2, Unit 3: Tell Me About It

# Quotation Marks

Follow these rules when you use quotation marks.

1. Put a **comma** after words such as *said* and *asked*.

2. Begin the first word inside the quotation marks with a **capital letter**.

3. Put the **end mark** inside the quotation marks.

Example: Jenna said, "I wrote a poem."

**Thinking Question**
*Where do the speaker's exact words begin and end?*

 **Draw a line under the sentence that is written correctly.**

**1.** Maddy asked, "Are you an artist?"

Maddy asked, "are you an artist?"

**2.** Jenna said "I am a writer."

Jenna said, "I am a writer."

**3.** Maddy asked, "Are poems hard to write?"

Maddy asked, "are poems hard to write?"

**4.** Jenna said, "poems are fun to write."

Jenna said, "Poems are fun to write."

# Focus Trait: Word Choice
# Use Exact Words

| Overused Words | Exact Words |
|---|---|
| Painting is a <u>fun</u> <u>thing</u>. | Painting is an **artistic hobby**. |

**A. Read each sentence on the left side. Add or change words to make them more exact.**

| Overused Words | Exact Words |
|---|---|
| **1.** Lunch is <u>the best part</u> of the day. | Lunch is _____ of the day. |
| **2.** At lunch, I can <u>talk</u> with <u>people</u>. | At lunch, I can _____ with _____. |

**B. Read each sentence with overused words. Add or change words to make them more exact. Write your new sentences.**

| Few Exact Words | Add Exact Words or Phrases |
|---|---|
| **3.** My art teacher is <u>good</u>. | |
| **4.** I love <u>making</u> <u>stuff</u>. | |

# Cumulative Review

Read each word. Add *-s* or *-es* to each base word.
Then write the new word.

1. rain _____

2. peach _____

3. train _____

4. pail _____

5. fox _____

6. wash _____

7. teach _____

8. catch _____

9. glass _____

10. stain _____

11. box _____

12. play _____

Name _____ Date _____

Lesson 13
PRACTICE BOOK

Schools Around
the World
Deepen Comprehension:
Author's Purpose

# Author's Purpose

**Read the selection below.**

No one really knows what schools of the future will look like. Perhaps school buildings will be high up in the clouds. That would save space on Earth. Children might get to school with a jet pack on their back, instead of a backpack!

Inside the classroom, everyone will surely have a computer, instead of books and a desk. That person in front of the class might be a robot, instead of a person. One thing probably will not change. That's homework!

**Complete an Inference Map about the author's purpose.**

| Schools may be high in the clouds. | | Classes in the future might not have teachers, books, or desks. |
|---|---|---|

Author's Purpose:

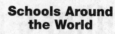

# Words with *ee, ea*

**Schools Around the World**

**Spelling:** Words with *ee, ea*

**Write two Spelling Words to complete each sentence.**

**1.** Use your _____ to chew when

you _____.

**2.** Will you _____ cover your

mouth when you _____?

**3.** We _____ wool from

_____ to make a sweater.

**4.** You can _____ the

_____ of a word in a dictionary.

**5.** The swimming _____ had a

race at the _____.

**6.** Ariana will _____ her friend

how to use a pottery _____.

**7.** During recess, we are _____ to

_____ about whatever we want.

| Spelling Words |
|---|
| **Basic Words** |
| 1. free |
| 2. teach |
| 3. teeth |
| 4. please |
| 5. beach |
| 6. wheel |
| 7. team |
| 8. speak |
| 9. sneeze |
| 10. sheep |
| 11. meaning |
| 12. weave |
| **Review Words** |
| 13. eat |
| 14. read |

Name _____ Date _____

Lesson 13
PRACTICE BOOK

Schools Around
the World
**Grammar:** Quotation Marks

# Quotation Marks

 **Write each sentence correctly.**

**1.** Mrs. Smith said, Artists mix colors.

_____

**2.** Greg said, I will mix blue and yellow.

_____

**3.** Annie said, You will make green!

_____

 **Draw a line under the sentence that is written correctly.**

**4.** Jamie said "I made a basket."

Jamie said, "I made a basket."

**5.** Robin asked, "how did you do it"?

Robin asked, "How did you do it?"

**6.** Jamie answered, "I made it out of straw."

Jamie answered ",I made it out of straw."

**Lesson 13**
PRACTICE BOOK

**Schools Around
the World**
**Vocabulary Strategies:**
Using a Dictionary

# Using a Dictionary

**Read the names for parts of a dictionary entry. Then
read the dictionary entry. Write in the boxes the labels
for the parts of the dictionary entry.**

**example sentence      part of speech      pronunciation**

**word meaning           entry word**

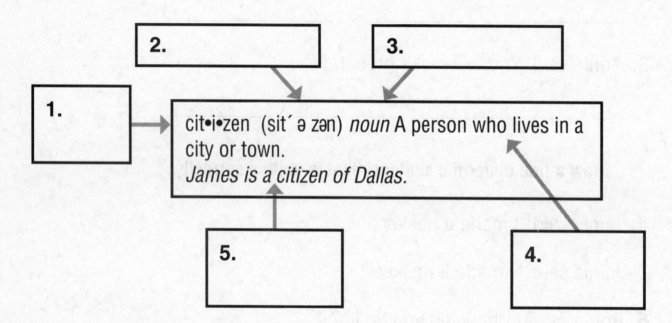

**6.** Write two good reasons to use a dictionary.

_____

_____

Name _____ Date _____

# Proofread for Spelling

**Proofread the letter. Circle the twelve misspelled words. Then write the correct spellings on the lines below.**

Dear Grandma,

We had a fun trip. Dad had to fix a weel on our car. Then we went to pet a shepe. The animals made Mom sneaz. We saw a girl weve a colorful rug. She tried to teech us the meening of each color.

At last we got to the beech. The shells were fre. I learned that some fish don't have any teeeth. We saw a volleyball teem. I got to spek to the players.

Well, that is all. Pleze write soon.

Love,
Tori

## Spelling Words

**Basic Words**
1. free
2. teach
3. teeth
4. please
5. beach
6. wheel
7. team
8. speak
9. sneeze
10. sheep
11. meaning
12. weave

1. _____
2. _____
3. _____
4. _____
5. _____
6. _____

7. _____
8. _____
9. _____
10. _____
11. _____
12. _____

# Action Verbs

Circle the verb.  Underline the subject that is doing the action.

1. Bobby jumps to his feet.

2. He dances to the music.

3. Sasha sings out loud.

4. They cheer for the band.

Underline the verb in the sentence.  Circle the verb that makes the action more exact.  Then write the new sentence.

5. The class made a picture.  (painted, watered)

_____

6. They used the brushes. (jumped, shared)

_____

7. Carla put the pictures on the wall.  (hung, walked)

_____

8. Children liked the artwork.  (saved, loved)

_____

Name _____ Date _____

Lesson 13
PRACTICE BOOK

Schools Around
the World
**Grammar:** Connect to Writing

# Conventions

| Sentences Written Incorrectly | Sentences Written Correctly |
|---|---|
| Jimmy asked "Is that a clay bowl?" Mom said. "yes, I made it in art class." | Jimmy asked, "Is that a clay bowl?" Mom said, "Yes, I made it in art class." |

**Write each sentence correctly. Fix mistakes in capitalization and punctuation. Put the quotation marks where they belong.**

**1.** Mom asked "Do you want to come to art class?

_____

**2.** I asked, what will we do?"

_____

**3.** "mom answered this week we will make puppets"

_____

**4.** I said "That sounds like fun!

_____

**5.** She said Next week we will put on a puppet show!"

_____

# Long *o (o, oa, ow)*

**Write a word for each clue.**

> **Word Bank**
>
> zero          clover          coast
> groan          gold          glow

**1.** It rhymes with **toast.**

It begins like **cap.** _____

**2.** It rhymes with **loan.**

It begins like **grapes.** _____

**3.** It rhymes with **fold.**

It begins like **gap.** _____

**4.** It rhymes with **show.**

It begins like **glad.** _____

**5.** It rhymes with **hero.**

It begins like **zip.** _____

**6.** It rhymes with **over.**

It begins like **clip.** _____

Name _____ Date _____

# Days of the Week

- There are seven days in a week.
- The names of the **days** of the week begin with **capital letters**.

| | | |
|---|---|---|
| **Monday** | **Thursday** | **Saturday** |
| **Tuesday** | **Friday** | **Sunday** |
| **Wednesday** | | |

Bonnie teaches sign language on <u>Tuesday</u>.

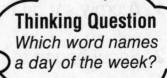

**Thinking Question**
*Which word names a day of the week?*

 **Write each sentence correctly.**

**1.** Bonnie teaches Jessica on wednesday.

_____

**2.** Jessica has a piano lesson on Tuesday.

_____

**3.** Jessica mails Bonnie a card on Friday.

_____

**4.** On monday Bonnie gets the card in the mail.

_____

**5.** On saturday Bonnie sends Jessica a card.

_____

# Long *o* (*o, oa, ow*)

**Read the sentences. Draw a circle around each word that has the long *o* sound spelled *o, oa,* or *ow*.**

**1.** A crow sat on the branch of the old oak tree.

**2.** Snow began to fall on a cold winter day.

**3.** Throw a stick in the water and see if it floats.

**4.** You can fold your own paper and put it away.

**5.** I know that the coach has a gold ring.

**Now write each word you circled under the word that has the same spelling for long *o*.**

| **told** | **loan** | **blow** |
|----------|----------|----------|
| _____ | _____ | _____ |
| _____ | _____ | _____ |
| _____ | _____ | _____ |
|          |          | _____ |

# Main Ideas and Details

We know that guide dogs can help blind people. But did you know that other trained animals can help people, too?

Service dogs are trained to help sick or injured people. If something falls, they can pick it up. They can pull a wheelchair. They can turn lights on and off. They can open and close doors. A service dog can also carry schoolbooks.

Monkeys can help people in wheelchairs. Trainers teach monkeys how to use their hands to do many things, such as get people something to eat or drink, pick up dropped items, help with CDs or videos, and turn lights on and off.

Life is better for many people because of animal helpers.

**Read the selection above. Then record supporting details below to tell more about the main idea shown.**

| **Main Idea:** Service animals can help sick or injured people. |
| --- |

# Long *o* (*o*, *oa*, *ow*)

**Helen Keller**
Spelling: Long *o* (*o*, *oa*, *ow*)

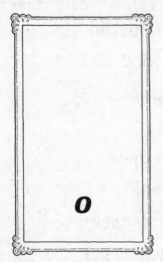

**o**          **oa**          **ow**

## Spelling Words

**Basic Words**
1. own
2. most
3. soap
4. float
5. both
6. know
7. loan
8. goat
9. flow
10. loaf
11. throw
12. coach

**Review Words**
13. so
14. grow

**Sort the Spelling Words by the long *o* sound, which can be spelled *o*, *oa*, or *ow*.**

| *o* Words | *oa* Words | *ow* Words |
|-----------|------------|------------|
| 1. _____ | 4. _____ | 10. _____ |
| 2. _____ | 5. _____ | 11. _____ |
| 3. _____ | 6. _____ | 12. _____ |
|  | 7. _____ | 13. _____ |
|  | 8. _____ | 14. _____ |
|  | 9. _____ |  |

**Underline the letter or letters in each word that make the long *o* sound.**

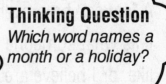
# Months of the Year and Holidays

> The names of **months** and **holidays** begin with **capital letters**.
>
> January   February   March   April
>
> May       June       July    August
>
> September October    November December
>
> Thanksgiving  Labor Day  Arbor Day
>
> In July, we celebrate Independence Day.

**Thinking Question**
*Which word names a month or a holiday?*

 **Write each underlined word correctly.**

**1.** Jan's School for the Blind opened in <u>february</u>.

_____

**2.** In <u>april</u>, Mom started working at the school.

_____

**3.** We have <u>memorial day</u> off from school.

_____

**4.** Every <u>july</u> the school has a picnic.

_____

**5.** <u>presidents' day</u> is in February.

_____

# Focus Trait: Ideas
# Facts and Opinions

A **fact** can be proved. An **opinion** cannot be proved. An opinion tells what someone thinks or feels. Words such as <u>I think</u>, <u>I like</u>, or <u>I believe</u> are used to show opinions.

**Read the paragraphs below. Write the opinion from each one. Write two facts that support each opinion.**

Helen Keller learned to read, write, and speak. I believe she was a remarkable person. She traveled around the world. She spoke to large crowds of people.

**Opinion:** _____

**Facts:** _____

_____

Annie Sullivan was Helen Keller's teacher. In the beginning, Helen fought with Annie. She even knocked out one of Annie's teeth. I think Helen was a real challenge for Annie.

**Opinion:** _____

**Facts:** _____

_____

# Cumulative Review

**Answer each pair of clues using the words below the clues.**

1. A place with sand by a lake or sea _____

   A big meal _____

   **beach**                    **feast**

2. Make a trip in a boat _____

   The feeling you have when you cut your hand

   _____

   **pain**                    **sail**

3. Show someone how to do something _____

   Stretch out your arm to grab something

   _____

   **teach**                    **reach**

4. How fast a car or truck is going _____

   A long way down under water _____

   **deep**                    **speed**

5. To stay in one place until something happens

   _____

   A path that you hike along _____

   **trail**                    **wait**

# Main Ideas and Details

**Read the selection below.**

Many tools help people who cannot see to share information. Since they can't see letters on a page, reading used to be impossible. But an inventor named Louis Braille gave each letter a different pattern of raised dots. A person can touch the dots and identify each letter. They put these letters together to form words and sentences. This way of reading is called Braille.

People can write with Braille displays. They type on a Braille display's keyboard. The Braille display turns this typing into words on the computer screen.

Screen readers are also helpful. Screen readers are computer programs that read words on a computer screen and then speak the words aloud.

**Complete the Idea-Support Map.**

**Main Idea:**

# Long *o (o, oa, ow)*

### Write the Spelling Word that matches each clue.

**1.** It cleans hands. _____

**2.** The biggest part _____

**3.** An animal that eats grass

_____

**4.** Something you do with a ball

_____

**5.** This person trains a team

_____

**6.** You get taller when you _____.

**7.** Two of something _____

**8.** A boat can _____.

**9.** When someone borrows money, it is a _____.

**10.** Water can _____ through a hose.

# Book Titles

> The first letter of each important word in a book title is capitalized. The entire title is underlined.

 **Write each book title correctly.**

**1.** The book diary of a spider made me laugh.

_____

**2.** I read henry and mudge yesterday.

_____

**3.** Did you like reading teacher's pets?

_____

 **Write each sentence correctly.**

**4.** Super storms was a great book.

_____

**5.** I read the book called my family.

_____

**6.** We all read schools around the world.

_____

Name _____ Date _____

# Suffix -*ly*

Add -*ly* to the base word to make a new word.  Write
the new word on the line.

**1.** sudden _____

**2.** soft _____

**3.** slow _____

**4.** warm _____

Choose the word from the box that completes the
sentence.  Write the word on the line.

> ### Word Bank
>
> happily        quickly        sadly

**5.** The girl smiled _____ when
she got the award.

**6.** I walked away _____ after we
said goodbye.

**7.** We were able to clean up _____
because we had lots of help.

# Proofread for Spelling

**Proofread Dan's report.  Circle the twelve misspelled words.
Then write the correct spellings on the lines below.**

I think baseball is the best game ever.  My team
is the Rams.  A ram is a gote with big horns.  Moast of
my friends are on my team.  Our coche teaches us to hit
and throa the ball.  You need to kno how to do bothe to
play.  You can't lofe at practice.  We practice throwing
until we make the ball floe from base to base.

I have my oan ball and glove.  Our hard hats are
on lon from the baseball club.  I like to run from base
to base.  I feel like I can flote on air.  Sometimes I slide
into a base.  When I get mud on my team shirt, Mom
cleans it with sop.

| | |
|---|---|
| Spelling Words | |
| **Basic Words** | |
| 1. own | |
| 2. most | |
| 3. soap | |
| 4. float | |
| 5. both | |
| 6. know | |
| 7. loan | |
| 8. goat | |
| 9. flow | |
| 10. loaf | |
| 11. throw | |
| 12. coach | |

1. _____    7. _____

2. _____    8. _____

3. _____    9. _____

4. _____    10. _____

5. _____    11. _____

6. _____    12. _____

# Present and Future Time

> • Add *-s* to the end of the verb when it tells about a noun that names one. Add *-es* to verbs ending with *s, x, ch,* and *sh* when they tell about a noun that names one.
>
> Examples: The boy <u>jumps</u>. The egg <u>hatches</u>.
>
> • Add *will* before the verb to tell about an action that will happen in the future.

 **Draw a line under the correct verb.**

**1.** The coach (teach, teaches) the girl.

**2.** The child (read, reads) in Braille.

**3.** The man (fix, fixes) their answers.

 **Write each sentence correctly to show future time.**

**4.** Carlos reach for a pen.

_____

**5.** Mary wash her hands before dinner.

_____

**6.** Ben pass the ball to me.

_____

# Ideas

| Without Words That Tell When | With Words That Tell When |
|---|---|
| Ben visits me. He hurt his leg. I made a card for him. | Ben visits me <u>every Saturday</u>. He hurt his leg <u>on June 12, 2010</u>. I made a card for him <u>on Valentine's Day</u>. |

✎ **Read the paragraph. Add phrases from the box to tell when. Write the phrases on the lines.**

> next Presidents' Day
> September 16
> last Thanksgiving
> every Thursday

Sarah lives next door. She teaches sign language. She started to teach on

_____, 2009. She teaches

two classes. Sarah also likes to help out at my

school. She did sign language for a school play

_____. She wants to do it again

for the play coming up _____.

# Compound Words

**Read the letter.  Draw a circle around each compound word.**

Dear Grandfather,

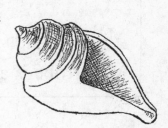

    This afternoon I went to the playground with some

kids from my classroom.  We played baseball until

sunset.  It was so much fun!  Then I went inside to do

my homework.  I went upstairs and saw the photo of us

at the seashore in the summertime.  I still have the

seashell we found there!

Love,<br>Julia

**Write a compound word you know on each line.**

_____    _____    _____

Name _____   Date _____

**Lesson 15**
PRACTICE BOOK

**Officer Buckle
and Gloria**
Grammar: Abbreviations

# Titles for People

- A **title** may be used before a person's name.
- A title begins with a capital letter and usually ends with a period.

Mr. Ramon is a music teacher.

Miss Kobe is a crossing guard.

**Thinking Question**
*Is there anything in front of the person's name?*

 **Write each underlined title and name correctly.**

**1.** Our teacher miss Mullin asks a police officer to visit.

_____

**2.** On Mondays mr Ramon comes to our class.

_____

**3.** He brings his partner, mrs Shay.

_____

**4.** They come with dr Lucky.

_____

**5.** They talk with the coach, ms Smith.

_____

Name _____ Date _____

**Lesson 15**
PRACTICE BOOK

**Officer Buckle
and Gloria**
**Phonics:** Compound Words

# Compound Words

**Find words in the box that go together to make compound words. Then make compound words to complete the sentences below. Read each completed sentence.**

> **Word Bank**
>
> pop    gold    sun    rain    snow    sail
> flake    boat    corn    bow    fish    shine

1. The _____ melted on my nose.

2. We saw a _____ in the sky

   after it rained.

3. _____ is a good snack to have

   in the afternoon.

4. It is fun to be on the lake in a _____.

5. Kate feeds her _____ twice a day.

6. The _____ felt warm on my face.

# Cause and Effect

Sam the Dog and Kelly the Cat were playing a game of catch. Sam was holding the ball in his paws.

"Get ready, Kelly!" yelled Sam.

He was just about to throw the ball when he tripped over a stick on the ground. The ball went flying into the air.

Kelly tried to catch the ball, but it bounced off her head and landed in a tree. Ed the Bird saw what had happened.

"Pardon me," Kelly said to Ed. "Would you help us get our ball out of the tree?"

"Of course," Ed chirped. Then he gave the ball a push. It fell to the ground.

"Thank you!" said Kelly and Sam together.

**Read the selection above. Complete a T-Map to show causes and effects.**

| Cause | Effect |
|---|---|
| **1.** | **1.** Sam trips. |
| **2.** The ball bounces off Kelly's head. | |
| **3.** | **3.** The ball lands on the ground. |

Name _____ Date _____

# Compound Words

Sort the Spelling Words by the number of letters in the first part of each compound word.

## Four Letters or More

1. _____

2. _____

3. _____

4. _____

## Three Letters

5. _____

6. _____

7. _____

8. _____

9. _____

## Two Letters

10. _____    13. _____

11. _____    14. _____

12. _____

### Spelling Words

**Basic Words**
1. cannot
2. pancake
3. maybe
4. baseball
5. playground
6. someone
7. myself
8. classroom
9. sunshine
10. outside
11. upon
12. nothing

**Review Words**
13. into
14. inside

Name _____ Date _____

**Lesson 15**
PRACTICE BOOK

Officer Buckle
and Gloria
**Grammar**: Abbreviations

# Abbreviations for Days and Months

- Each day of the week can be written in a short way, called an **abbreviation**.

**Mon. Tues. Wed. Thurs. Fri. Sat. Sun.**

- Some months of the year can also be written in a short way. Notice that May, June, and July do not have a shortened form

| | | |
|---|---|---|
| **Jan.** | **May** | **Sept.** |
| **Feb.** | **June** | **Oct.** |
| **Mar.** | **July** | **Nov.** |
| **Apr.** | **Aug.** | **Dec.** |

The first Tues. in Mar.

**Thinking Question**
*What does the short form of the word look like?*

**Write the abbreviation for each word.**

**1.** Wednesday _____

**2.** December _____

**3.** Sunday _____

**4.** January _____

**5.** Monday _____

**6.** March _____

**7.** September _____

**8.** Tuesday _____

**9.** November _____

**10.** Saturday _____

**11.** February _____

**12.** July _____

**13.** June _____

**14.** October _____

**15.** Thursday _____

**16.** August _____

**17.** Friday _____

**18.** April _____

Name _____ Date _____

**Lesson 15**
PRACTICE BOOK

**Officer Buckle
and Gloria**
**Writing**: Write to Persuade

# Focus Trait: Organization
# Topic Sentences

> A good persuasive essay has a goal, reasons, and facts and examples. The **goal** is what the writer wants. **Reasons** tell why. **Facts** and **examples** give more information about the reason.

**Read the persuasive essay. Write the goal. Circle the reasons. Underline facts and examples.**

## Why We Need Officer Buckle and Gloria

I have a great idea! Officer Buckle and Gloria should speak at our school.

One reason is that we all need to learn about safety. Safety tips can keep us from hurting ourselves. They can even save lives!

Another reason is that Officer Buckle and Gloria put on a great show! Gloria acts out all the safety tips. Kids love watching Gloria!

So please, let's invite Officer Buckle and Gloria to speak at our school. I think it would be great!

**Goal:** _____

**What reason does the second paragraph tell about?**

_____

_____

Name _____ Date _____

**Lesson 15**
PRACTICE BOOK

**Officer Buckle
and Gloria**
**Phonics:** Schwa Vowel Sound

# Schwa Vowel Sound

**Write each word. Draw a slash (/) to divide the word between syllables.
Then circle the quieter syllable with the schwa sound.**

1. happen _____

2. about _____

3. talent _____

4. nickel _____

5. alone _____

6. dragonfly _____

**Now use the words you wrote above to complete the
sentences below.**

7. Luis has a lot of _____ for singing.

8. Sometimes Mia likes to be _____.

9. A _____ flew by.

10. What will _____ if it rains

    during the game?

11. Stan paid a _____ for a gumball.

12. Tell me _____ the picture you made.

Name _____ Date _____

**Lesson 15**
PRACTICE BOOK

**Officer Buckle
and Gloria**
**Deepen Comprehension:**
Cause and Effect

# Cause and Effect

**Read the selection below.**

Tim was great at taking pictures. That's why Maya asked
for his help. She wanted to enter a picture of her dog Rex into
the Pet Photo Contest. "I'll have Rex do a trick as you take
the picture," Maya said.

"Great idea!" Tim replied. Rex wagged his tail.

Everybody walked to the tennis courts. Rex stood on one
side of the net, and Maya stood on the other.

"Here, Rex!" Maya said. She held up a dog treat. Rex
ran and jumped over the net as Tim clicked his camera.

"I got Rex jumping in the air!" Tim said. He showed the
picture to Maya. "This photo will be a winner for sure!"

**Complete a T-Map to show cause and effect.**

| Cause | Effect |
|---|---|
| 1. | 1. Maya asked for Tim's help. |
| 2. | 2. They went to the tennis courts. |
| 3. Maya pulled out a dog treat. | 3. |
| 4. | 4. Tim thought the picture could win the contest. |

# Compound Words

Draw lines to match the words that form Spelling Words.
Then write the Spelling Words.

| play | self |
|------|------|
| sun | to |
| my | ground |
| in | shine |
| some | not |
| can | one |
| out | side |

| pan | thing |
|-----|-------|
| no | cake |
| may | on |
| base | be |
| class | side |
| up | ball |
| in | room |

**Spelling Words**

**Basic Words**
1. cannot
2. pancake
3. maybe
4. baseball
5. playground
6. someone
7. myself
8. classroom
9. sunshine
10. outside
11. upon
12. nothing

**Review Words**
13. into
14. inside

1. _____
2. _____
3. _____
4. _____
5. _____
6. _____
7. _____

8. _____
9. _____
10. _____
11. _____
12. _____
13. _____
14. _____

# Abbreviations for Places

✏️ **Write each underlined place correctly. Use abbreviations.**

**1.** I live on <u>Robin Road</u>.

_____

**2.** The pool is on <u>Shore drive</u>.

_____

**3.** Where is <u>Third avenue</u>?

_____

✏️ **Write the name of the underlined words correctly. Write each abbreviation in its long form.**

**4.** Max lives on <u>North St</u>.

_____

**5.** Gloria visited a school on <u>Elm Ave</u>.

_____

**6.** <u>Rose Rd.</u> is only two blocks long.

_____

Name _____ Date _____

# Dictionary Entry

Look at the guide words on the dictionary pages below.
Then look at the entry words in the large box. Write each
entry word in the box that has the correct guide words.

| sad / snow |
| --- |
| _____ |
| _____ |

| thirty / tick |
| --- |
| _____ |
| _____ |

| bake / bump |
| --- |
| _____ |
| _____ |

| dentist / enough |
| --- |
| _____ |
| _____ |

**banner** – a long strip of cloth with a message on it

**bulletin** – a short news report

**department** – a section of a large store

**enormous** – very large

**safety** – the state of being safe from danger

**snore** – to breathe loudly while sleeping

**thought** – an idea or opinion

**thumbtack** – a small pin you can push into a wall

# Proofread for Spelling

**Proofread these sentences.  Circle the misspelled words.
Then write the correct spellings on the lines below.**

1. Wear sunscreen when you are owtside in the
   sunsheen.

   _____    _____

2. You canut throw things in your clasroom.

   _____    _____

3. Let somone help you cook a pancak.

   _____    _____

4. To protect miself, I wear a bike helmet uppon my head.

   _____    _____

5. Nutting should be close by when you hit a basbal.

   _____    _____

6. Mayby we can go to the plagrownd on Sunday.

   _____    _____

<table>
<tr><td colspan="2">**Spelling Words**</td></tr>
</table>

## Basic Words
1. cannot
2. pancake
3. maybe
4. baseball
5. playground
6. someone
7. myself
8. classroom
9. sunshine
10. outside
11. upon
12. nothing

**Lesson 15**
PRACTICE BOOK

**Officer Buckle
and Gloria**
**Grammar:** Spiral Review

# Past and Future Tenses

✏️  **Write each sentence to change when the action
happened. Use the word in ( ).**

**1.** The police officers talk about safety. (past)

_____

**2.** The children listen to them. (future)

_____

**3.** They follow the rules. (future)

_____

✏️  **Read the story.  Find five verbs that do not tell about
the past, and fix them.  Write the story correctly on the lines.**

The policeman and his dog walked to the school.
They wait at the front door.  Then the dog bark.  The
principal open the door.  The policeman talk with the
children about safety.  The children thank him.

_____

_____

_____

_____

# Conventions

| Incorrect Abbreviations | Correct Abbreviations |
|---|---|
| dr levi | Dr. Levi |
| ms Jones | Ms. Jones |
| miss Oaks | Miss Oaks |
| River st | River St. |
| Tues | Tues. |
| jan. | Jan. |

**Proofread the paragraph. Fix any mistakes in abbreviations. Write the paragraph correctly on the lines.**

My dad is a teacher. Kids call him mr Gary. On tues Dad read to his class. In mar they studied butterflies. Then on fri they visited a butterfly show. The show was on Main st.

_____

_____

_____

_____

_____

_____

**225**